GHOST

Berkley titles by Glenn Puit

WITCH:
THE TRUE STORY OF LAS VEGAS'S MOST
NOTORIOUS FEMALE KILLER

FATHER OF THE YEAR:
BILL RUNDLE: ALL-AMERICAN JEKYLL AND HYDE

IN HER PRIME:
THE MURDER OF A POLITICAL STAR

GHOST:
THE TRUE STORY OF ONE MAN'S DESCENT INTO
MADNESS AND MURDER

GHOST

The True Story of One Man's Descent
into Madness and Murder

GLENN PUIT

BERKLEY BOOKS, NEW YORK

THE BERKLEY PUBLISHING GROUP
Published by the Penguin Group
Penguin Group (USA) Inc.
375 Hudson Street, New York, New York 10014, USA
Penguin Group (Canada), 90 Eglinton Avenue East, Suite 700, Toronto, Ontario M4P 2Y3, Canada
(a division of Pearson Penguin Canada Inc.)
Penguin Books Ltd., 80 Strand, London WC2R 0RL, England
Penguin Group Ireland, 25 St. Stephen's Green, Dublin 2, Ireland (a division of Penguin Books Ltd.)
Penguin Group (Australia), 250 Camberwell Road, Camberwell, Victoria 3124, Australia
(a division of Pearson Australia Group Pty. Ltd.)
Penguin Books India Pvt. Ltd., 11 Community Centre, Panchsheel Park, New Delhi—110 017, India
Penguin Group (NZ), 67 Apollo Drive, Rosedale, North Shore 0632, New Zealand
(a division of Pearson New Zealand Ltd.)
Penguin Books (South Africa) (Pty.) Ltd., 24 Sturdee Avenue, Rosebank, Johannesburg 2196,
South Africa

Penguin Books Ltd., Registered Offices: 80 Strand, London WC2R 0RL, England

The publisher does not have any control over and does not assume any responsibility for author or third-party websites or their content.

GHOST

A Berkley Book / published by arrangement with the author

PRINTING HISTORY
Berkley mass-market edition / January 2011

ISBN: 978-0-425-24012-0

BERKLEY®
Berkley Books are published by The Berkley Publishing Group,
a division of Penguin Group (USA) Inc.,
375 Hudson Street, New York, New York 10014.
BERKLEY® is a registered trademark of Penguin Group (USA) Inc.
The "B" design is a trademark of Penguin Group (USA) Inc.

PRINTED IN THE UNITED STATES OF AMERICA

10 9 8 7 6 5 4 3 2 1

Most Berkley Books are available at special quantity discounts for bulk purchases for sales, promotions, premiums, fund-raising, or educational use. Special books, or book excerpts, can also be created to fit specific needs.

For details, write: Special Markets, The Berkley Publishing Group, 375 Hudson Street, New York, New York 10014.

This book is dedicated to my mother,
Dolores Hicks,
who lives in Upstate New York;
to Greg and Sandy Chopp of Michigan's Upper
Peninsula;
and also to my colleagues
at the Michigan Land Use Institute.
They have stuck with me through the three
most difficult years of my life, 2008–2010,
and I am forever grateful for all of their love,
guidance, and support. I will never forget it.

INTRODUCTION

My name is Glenn Puit. I witnessed human cruelty and evil at its darkest levels in my seventeen years of work in the print media news business. I covered violent crime and capital murder trials in Las Vegas from 1996 to 2007 for the *Las Vegas Review-Journal*, and I wrote, every day, about the most heinous crimes imaginable in Sin City. A psychotic man who shot four innocent strangers to death as they shopped for groceries. A horrifically cruel quadruple murder in which four promising young men were tied up and shot to death for a hundred-plus bucks, a pager, and a video-game player. A cab driver doused with gasoline and set on fire in a robbery for a few hundred dollars, or the lethal stabbing of a child and the paralyzing of another over the selling of a bag of salt in a drug deal.

The experiences covering crime in Las Vegas and also in South Carolina have, of course, left me incredibly appreciative of life. I've always covered crime because I believe life is precious, and I hope that by my telling these stories, we can all be a little bit more aware and mindful of the fact that in this beautiful world—where humans do great good—evil walks among us.

This is a common thread in my true-crime books. My first book, *Witch*, chronicles the story of a successful, seemingly normal technical writer who killed her mother and stored her in a storage shed for three years. *Father of the Year* details the life of a man once voted "Father of the Year" in Las Vegas. In actuality, he was a coldhearted killer. And in my book *In Her Prime*, a talented critical-care nurse who seemed to have everything going for him poisoned his wife in the most cruel way. The message I try to convey through these books is this: always be careful in life and be wary of evil. It is out there, and there is no better evidence of this than the book you have in your hands right now.

The origins of this book stem from my work as a reporter at the *Las Vegas Review-Journal* from 2002 to 2006. I was assigned in 2002 to cover the criminal case of John Patrick Addis—a man on the lam for nearly a decade in the killing of Las Vegan Joann Albanese.

What I would learn about Addis as I reviewed court files and conducted interviews is that Addis was a controlling, obsessive, cold-blooded killer. However, he was also more than just a killer: he was a very smart man trained in law enforcement and wilderness survival. He was incredibly elusive and was always one step ahead of authorities. He is one of the most intriguing criminals I've ever come across, and he is arguably the most complex and interesting killer in Las Vegas history. I think you will agree with that assessment after you read this book.

Addis is a person who thrives on complete control and a very vile form of domestic violence. He victimizes people who dare to try to break free from the control. He is a very scary human being, and what makes him so scary is his normalcy. Meeting Addis and shaking his hand and talking to him would never reveal to you just how evil a person he was. You usually didn't get to see the pure evil of Addis until you were close to him.

I always knew while covering the story in Las Vegas that the case would make a great book. I always promised myself that, if I got the chance, I was going to write it.

Several people who I reached out to for interviews declined my requests. I respect their decision to do so. I recognize that Addis's actions have caused immense pain and suffering to many, and anyone who knows me knows I spent my entire newspaper career sticking up for victims of violent crime and their families, so again, I respect their choice. I have a very real understanding of the wreckage Addis left behind in Alaska, Las Vegas, and Mexico. So, to the victims' families and those forever affected by Addis, I offer my sincerest and most heartfelt condolences and a great desire that you are able to find peace and strength in the face of such devastation.

Researching this book was also not easy. I've been threatened with a lawsuit and asked to pay for interviews—requests I always refuse. I've pushed forward because I believe in the power of journalism. I am a firsthand witness to the ability of journalism to educate, inform, and even change the world. I write these books for that very reason—to give people knowledge about the small percentage of people out there who spend most of their lives victimizing others. It is a valuable lesson each of us needs to be reminded of regularly: be thankful for what you've got—be thankful for being alive—and be very careful about trusting others until they've demonstrated they are worthy of that trust.

I have used pseudonyms for the names of several witnesses contained in police reports and Alaska court records. These pseudonyms are denoted by asterisks.

So, as I sit here, wrapping up this very difficult project, a few thank-yous are in order for those who made this all possible. Thanks to my editors at Berkley, Shannon Jamieson-Vasquez and Faith Black. I'm honored to write for Berkley. Thanks to my literary agent, Jim Cypher, who has guided me through the pitfalls and challenges of writing five books in as many years while working very demanding full-time jobs. Thanks to Las Vegas police detective Larry Hanna. He greatly assisted me in my research. Thanks to all the Alaska law enforcement officers and officials who granted me interviews and provided me a great deal of insight into Addis's unraveling in that state. Thanks to my researcher, Timothy Pratt, formerly of the *Las Vegas Sun*, who helped me explore Addis's time in Mexico. Thanks to Alaska judge Jane Kauvar. She took the time to guide me through the Alaskan criminal justice system when I faced obstacle after obstacle. Thanks to all the public library researchers in Alaska, Michigan, and Montana. They took the time to assist me when they had no obligation to do so. Thanks to veteran Alaska journalist Kris Capps and Las Vegas Court Information Officer Michael Sommermeyer. Thanks to Las Vegan Sam Morris and *Review-Journal* photo editor Jeff Scheid, who each helped me obtain additional photos for this book when I was in a pinch because of a problem with my photo-scanning software. I want to thank my friends at the Michigan Land Use Institute in Traverse City. They are great people.

Most importantly, though, I want to thank you, the reader. Thanks for reading my books and giving me your support.

—Glenn Puit

1 . . . JOANN

The great American city of Las Vegas basically got its start because of a couple of narrow streams of crystal clear spring water. The naturally occurring streams in what is now known as the Las Vegas Valley were a gathering spot for Native Americans. The streams cobbled together in nature's glorious, captivating, and mysterious ways a marshy and grassy area in the middle of the desert. John C. Frémont, the nineteenth-century explorer, traveled through here as he sought to chart the Americas and the expansive West. Trappers and traders made the marshy area a stop on the Old Spanish Trail. The Mormons used the area as a stopping point in their journey across the country.

Around the turn of the century, the railroads took over in Las Vegas. By 1905, a railroad track ran through downtown Las Vegas, and the connection to California was made. In 1931, the state legalized gambling, leading to the eventual boom of the great city of Las Vegas.

Today, the city has two personalities. The first is pure Americana. A gargantuan stretch of suburbia runs from one end of the Las Vegas Valley to the other. There are stucco homes, strip malls, parks, and golf courses. The expansive skies hovering over the city are big, blue, and wide open. It snows maybe once every five years or so in Vegas, and it gets below 50 degrees just a few times a year. There's lots of sun, and it almost never rains. Homes are cheap again in Las Vegas after the Great Recession crushed the city's economy in 2008. The city still offers everything from lounge acts to headliner shows at Strip resorts featuring, over the years, the likes of Elvis, the Rat Pack, and Wayne Newton. The city can be a great place to raise a family, as well, if you pick the right neighborhood. There are good schools, it's safe, and there are good people everywhere. Las Vegas can be a truly charming place to live.

But the city—Sin City—also has another side. It's the dark side, and the dark side has a completely different personality. It is a ruthless one. Pickpockets. Hustlers. Drunks. Drug addicts. Methamphetamine tweakers. Gambling freaks on endless losing streaks.

Predators.

The Lakes community in northwest Las Vegas is a nice place. It's not the type of place where people just disappear.

The Lakes serves as an oasis for middle-income to upper-class Las Vegans fatigued by the grind and bustle of Sin City. You can't walk to The Lakes if you are in

downtown Las Vegas or on the Strip. You have to drive.
You hop on the interstate and battle the race-car-like traffic
headed north and west until you hop off the interstate and
pass the Starbucks, the strip malls, the payday loan opera-
tions, the pawnshops, the Walmarts, the grocery stores, the
schools, the lush parks, and the huge American flags that
drape from gigantic, three-story flagpoles at convenience
stores in suburban Las Vegas. You wind your way through
a series of six-lane roadways, perfectly squared intersec-
tions, and stoplights until you get to the base of a hill. As
your car climbs upward, you suddenly notice you've left
the dusty, sunbaked concrete of Vegas for the world of The
Lakes.

Huge palm and assorted blossoming trees offer shade in
a two-square-mile, master-planned community that sits a
few miles from the rusty escarpments of the Spring Mountains to the west. There are nice patches of dark green
grass, and sprinkler mist hangs in the air. The Lakes is
a stretch of some four thousand white, tan, or yellowish
stucco homes with red-clay roof shingles. The homes sur-
round sizable manmade lakes, and the feature lake of The
Lakes community, to the north of the property, certainly
doesn't look like it's manmade. The water in the lake is
very blue. There are palm trees everywhere. A recreation
center on the edge of the lake is a big hit in the community,
and there is a jogging trail that encircles the entire lake.
Geese at the end of the jogging trail waddle back and forth
from the lake to the jogging trail and peck at joggers who
dare to get too close.

The Lakes is a quality community in a big city with all

the traditional big-city problems and challenges, and it is
the community Joann Albanese called home in 1995. The
single mother of two cherished daughters was born Joann
Greenrock on January 20, 1956, in Bussac, France, into
a military family. Joann's mother, Margarete Greenrock,
was a doting mother to Joann, and her father was a U.S.
Army veteran. Joann's sister, Dollie, is one year older than
Joann.

The Greenrock family lived the military life early on,
going from barracks to barracks and base to base. They
were stationed in Germany for three years before returning to the States. Joann's parents eventually divorced, and
Joann, her sister, and her mother subsequently spent most
of their lives in Las Vegas. And despite it being Sin City,
Joann was like most people who live in Vegas—she was
a moral, honest person, and she was particularly close to
her mother. Margarete was a gentle beacon of stability for
Joann and Dollie. Joann and Margarete spoke almost daily,
and they shared with one another the most personal details
of life. Margarete Greenrock was a conservative woman of
small stature who spoke fluent German. Margarete loved
her daughters more than life itself, and she couldn't ever
imagine having children better than Joann and Dollie.
Margarete described Joann as an excellent student and a
beautiful child who never gravitated to drinking or drugs,
and she kept in constant contact with her mother at Margarete's modest Las Vegas home.

"Very close," Margarete would later say of the mother-
daughter relationship in testimony offered to a Las Vegas
grand jury. "She was a good daughter, excellent daughter.
She didn't drink. She didn't smoke, and two or three times

a day, I talked to her. Sometimes four times a day on the phone. We were very attached to each other."

Joann took up fashion modeling while a junior at Western High School in Vegas. Fashion modeling was a good fit because Joann was a very beautiful young lady who became a very beautiful woman. She had dark hair that dropped down to her shoulders. Sometimes she wore it curly. Other times, she wore it in a big, straight cut that was typical of the mid-1990s. She had intense, dark eyes and an attractive smile, and she was very classy. Her demeanor was genteel, graceful, and refined. She wore her makeup in a way that gave her face a dark, glowing, and majestic luster to complement her dark eyes. She had nice tastes, too. She liked to stay in the finest hotels while traveling. She liked the feeling of walking into a luxurious hotel entryway and seeing the history of the place. She liked the feeling of unlocking a door and walking into an environment of ease. The beds were perfectly made. The service was perfect, and she was catered to. There was often an elegant view of international cityscape or beach outside her hotel room in her travels, and this gave Joann peace and sanctity.

Joann enjoyed dining in nice restaurants. Joann loved jewelry, bracelets, and earrings, and these possessions were especially important to her. Each piece represented a time in her life in which she'd received the gift of love—the rings, necklace, and bracelets were given to her by family, and they were close to her heart. She loved holding the items in her hands and thinking about the time it took to make the pieces. She loved the look of sparkling diamonds and glistening gold. Each piece, to Joann, was a work of art, like an alluring painting or an enticing sculpture.

Joann's loved ones would later tell police she only took her favorite pieces of jewelry off when she was in the shower. As soon as she jumped out of the shower, the jewelry was right back on.

Joann met a man she came to love very dearly when she was just sixteen. Thomas Albanese was a new graduate of Western High School, and he found Joann to be an incredibly smart, talented, and beautiful woman. Tom is a very gentle soul. He's an ambitious person and a very hard worker. The couple married in 1976, and the two set about building a life together. Tom went into food service and became an extremely successful restaurant products distributor. Joann, meanwhile, did fashion modeling from 1973 to 1975, and she then worked as a sales manager at Harriette's Women's Apparel Boutique in Las Vegas for two years. Next, she worked as a secretary and leasing agent at Marie Antoinette Condominiums in Vegas. Tom and Joann wanted to have children, and in 1978, their first daughter, Amber, was born. The couple's second daughter, Brittany, came seven years later, and Joann loved her daughters dearly. She viewed both of her children as incredible blessings from God, and Joann loved being a mom. It was her whole world, and Tom Albanese later noted how remarkable a mother Joann was to her daughters.

"Very loving," he said. "Very attentive to their needs, and [she] was very protective. Very protective, and always was in touch."

The couple bought a house in The Lakes in 1983 because it was one of the nicest communities in Las Vegas. They bought a two-story, Spanish-style home—with three bedrooms, a separate family room, formal dining room, kitchen, breakfast nook, and living room. The home had a swimming pool and was fully landscaped in the front and the back, and it offered a covered patio in the backyard. It was an elegant home. Tom Albanese was making a nice living brokering foods from distributors to restaurants in the city, and Joann spent most of her days taking care of her two daughters. The family traveled extensively on their vacations, and Joann enjoyed these experiences immensely. Over time, the couple and their children globe-trotted all over the world for conventions and resort stays. Joann, it seemed, lived for the thrill of jumping on an airplane at McCarran International Airport in Vegas and going somewhere—anywhere in the world—on junkets that temporarily allowed her to escape from her day-to-day existence in Las Vegas. She loved getting away from the heat of Sin City and spending time in a different environment with the man and children she loved.

"I enjoy traveling and do so frequently," Joann once wrote in a résumé entered into evidence during a grand jury proceeding following her disappearance. "My personal travels include the majority of the United States, including Alaska and Hawaii. [I've also been to] Canada, Mexico, Caribbean, Australia, Africa, Asia, and throughout Europe."

Joann's love of travel soon evolved into a career pursuit: she took a part-time job as a travel agent. She worked as an independent agent at Fantastic Journey Travel and Tours in northwest Las Vegas. She served dozens of individual Las Vegans and corporate accounts regularly, booking their airline tickets, tours, cruises, rail tickets, hotel reservations, and car rentals. Joann marketed herself on her résumé as an agent "that specializes in the international and domestic markets," and she traveled to St. Louis, Kansas City, and California to take classes on reservation booking and computers offered by Trans World and United Airlines.

It seemed like the perfect life for the couple, but by the late 1980s, the marriage was falling apart. Tom and Joann fought frequently, and Joann was known to have a fiery side to her personality. She was, in fact, a person who let people know what she thought, and the Las Vegas police detectives who would later investigate her disappearance said Joann wouldn't hold back when she felt she'd been wronged. In one instance, Las Vegas police tell of an incident in which Joann showed up at the Las Vegas police juvenile hall detail to complain about a minor police contact with her daughter Amber and tore into every cop in front of her at the Juvenile Detective Division. She was furious, and her tirade prompted more than one person in the juvenile section to specifically remember Joann and her temper after her disappearance.

Tom and Joann Albanese officially divorced in 1991, and Joann received some beneficial terms from the divorce. She received primary custody of their daughters, with Tom Albanese having visitation every weekend. Per the couple's divorce decree in December 1991, Tom Albanese paid Joann one thousand dollars a month per child for child support. He also paid one thousand dollars per month to Joann in spousal support, for a total of three thousand a month. Joann was awarded the home in The Lakes as part of the divorce proceedings as well, and it was a valuable asset. The home, appraised at one hundred and ten thousand dollars, was estimated to have forty-five to fifty-five thousand dollars in equity. The divorce was not hostile, but it was not warm either, and the two, despite their differences, committed themselves to caring for the children in a way that served both their daughters. The contact between Tom Albanese and his ex was not extensive, however, and there was a frostiness to the relationship following the divorce. Tom Albanese said he and his ex-wife had little interest in chatting with one another, and as a result, the two figured out a rigid schedule for exchanging the children. They made sure, though, to talk to one another if the schedule for exchanging the children ever needed to be altered. The two often exchanged the children at the family's old home on Coast Walk in The Lakes or at Tom Albanese's home nearby.

"I saw her just briefly," Tom Albanese would later tell a Las Vegas grand jury of the custody exchanges. "Unless there were some issues with Brittany or Amber not feeling well, and I needed to get medication from her, [Joann] would just drop the kids off after she made sure that I was there."

Albanese would tell a Las Vegas grand jury that any changes the couple had to visitation rights were clearly communicated so each parent would have "as much lead time" as possible. Albanese even wrote down the details of any incidents in which he gave advance notice to his wife over changes to parenting time. Other than communications over parenting time or an emergency, he said, the communication between the couple "was hardly ever."

The two needed to stick to their schedule of exchanging the children, given the lack of communication. They stuck to the schedule religiously, and their child exchanges became so routine for the two that Tom Albanese could drop the children off at the home in The Lakes on a Sunday afternoon, and he just knew Joann would be inside. She was always there waiting for the children.

Joann was that dependable.

"It was our habit, absolutely," Tom Albanese said.

By late 1994, Amber Albanese, like her mother, had grown into a very beautiful young lady. The fifteen-year-old had brown hair and was sweet. She was, however, struggling in a divorced family, and she rebelled at times. There were instances when she clashed with her mother, and the clashes were typical of most mother-and-daughter disputes when the daughter enters her teenage years.

"My daughter, my oldest daughter, was experiencing problems with her mother, as she was with me," Tom Albanese would later tell a Las Vegas grand jury. "She was going through a stage; you know, she was a rebel. And Joann was having some difficulties with her, and I offered her to take both girls, and nothing ever came of it."

Joann had big hopes and dreams for both her daughters. The mother and daughters were close. Joann and Amber and Brittany were like Joann and Margarete—they were mother and daughters, and their blood bond meant they were there for one another forever. They cared about each other, they worried about each other, and they looked out for one another.

Joann, at the same time, was struggling with being a single mom. She was alone in the world and responsible for two girls, and it was hard. Joann was a strong woman, and she had a very strong desire to make a life for herself outside of the homemaker and mother existence she'd known during her time with her ex-husband. Being a mom was her whole life—the most important thing to her—but now she wanted more. She'd married her husband right out of high school, and she'd envisioned that marriage, and her family, being the very center of her existence forever. Joann knew, though, that she had to move on when she divorced Tom Albanese. In 1993, Joann learned about the imminent opening of the grandest hotel in Las Vegas at the time—the MGM Grand Hotel & Casino. The massive structure at Tropicana Avenue and Las Vegas Boulevard on the Strip was going to be the hottest place in town, and Joann saw an opportunity to find some meaningful work at the property when it opened. On June 10, 1993, she wrote the MGM Grand's community resources director, Tony Gladney, to ask for a job.

"Recently I learned through Janice Mace of Nevada Employment Security Department of your recruitment to hire and train employees for your new resort," Joann wrote. "If you will be interviewing for mid or upper management in the areas of front desk operation, reservations, personal assistant or public relations representative, I would appreciate [you] considering me.

"I have extensive background in the travel industry, have a broad knowledge of the needs of our tourist community and excellent public contact experience," Joann wrote. "For your review I am enclosing a résumé of my qualifications. I would appreciate an opportunity to complete your company application and a personal interview with you to discuss my qualifications and interest. Thanking you in advance for your time and consideration. Sincerely, Joann Albanese."

Officials at the MGM were impressed with Joann, and she was quickly offered a job at the Strip property. She was an in-house business consultant at the gaming property and helped organize trips and junkets to the property for tourists. It was a good, solid job that Joann cherished.

Joann continued to work part-time as a travel agent, too, but she was constantly exhausted with what proved to be a rigorous schedule. Only a single parent knows how hard it is to work full-time and care for two kids. Up at 6 a.m. Breakfast for the girls. Get the girls ready and off to school. A full day's work at the MGM. Get home, exhausted, and still find the time to be a loving, patient mom to her kids. By 1995, Joann Albanese was clearly looking for something more in her life, and she told friends she worried she might spend the rest of her existence alone. She dated and was in a couple of relationships after her divorce, but none worked out. She craved a relationship with a good-looking, honest man who cared for her and loved her, and she wanted a man who wouldn't be bothered by the fact that she had two children. Joann was a single, attractive, classy woman, and she got some steady interest from men, but Joann was picky. She only liked men who were good-looking and strong. She liked men who were physically fit and confident. She didn't want any partiers who drank, did drugs, or hung out in strip clubs chasing strippers.

There was plenty of that kind of man in Vegas.

Friends said Joann was a beautiful, elegant woman who would be a great catch for a man, yet when it came to men, they thought Joann was a little too self-conscious about her appearance. She had a beautiful face and figure, but she regularly told friends in Las Vegas she was concerned about her age, weight, and looks. She tried to get to the gym at least a couple of times a week. Friends told her she was a total catch for a good man, but she still worried about her appearance.

Around the same time, Joann's closest friend, Tara Rivera, had just joined the World's Gym in Las Vegas for the same reasons. Rivera is a woman of small stature, and after having kids, she wanted to drop a few pounds. Rivera is a gentle woman with dark hair and a dark complexion. She'd worked at the MGM with Joann since 1993, and the two struck up a friendship. They became very close: the best of friends. Rivera often counseled Joann, and Rivera—along with Joann's mother and her sister, Dollie—were the ones who served as Joann's support system. Rivera said she talked regularly with Joann about finding a new man, and Rivera was routinely on the lookout for a man who might be a good match for her friend.

In April of 1995, that man appeared seemingly out of nowhere. Rivera had just signed up for some personal-fitness lessons at the World's Gym, and the personal trainer assigned to her was a man by the name of John Edwards. Rivera was struck almost immediately by Edwards's good looks and soft nature. He was one of those men who was blessed by God with charisma and exceedingly good looks. From a distance, he was stunning—the type of man who would seem to have no problem whatsoever getting women.

His face was chiseled. He had a very strong jaw, granite-like, and deep green eyes. He seemed rugged yet clean-cut, with smooth skin and a well-groomed appearance. His hair was blond and parted, giving him a movie-star-like facial profile, and he was tanned and toned like a bodybuilder. He was a big man with a muscular, very strong physique. He walked confidently yet seemed soft and kind from the moment you met him. He was single with no kids. Those who knew him said he gave the impression that he cared about people, and Tara thought Edwards was the perfect fit for Joann.

"I was working out at the time, and they assigned [John] to go through the gym with me, and he became a personal trainer," Rivera recalled.

Rivera went through a couple of personal-training sessions with Edwards. It was clear he knew a lot about fitness. He was an expert in staying fit through a combination of cardio, weights, and proper diet. Edwards was clearly a very strong man who had spent a lot of time in his life working to maintain his level of physical fitness. The man spoke with great authority about human health. Edwards told Rivera he was from Florida, that he'd managed a string of fitness centers there, and that he'd moved to Las Vegas to rebuild his life after becoming estranged from his family. He was outgoing, charming, personable, and caring.

"I thought he was a great guy," Rivera would later recall for a Las Vegas grand jury. "A perfect guy for [Joann]. He was forty-five, single, never been married. . . . She had so much going for her, and I thought they'd make a great couple."

"I introduced them somewhere around March or April," Rivera said. "Soon after, they started dating, and they just became very close."

Just four months later, Joann Albanese would seemingly vanish off the face of the earth. She went missing, leaving hardly a trace of evidence behind, and it would take three tortuous, pain-filled years for her family to find out what really happened to her.

2 ... MICHIGAN

Michigan, with all its natural beauty, wildlife, and incredible hunting grounds, is the state John Patrick Addis was born and raised in, and it is a place that would remain in his blood forever.

Michigan is a sportsman's dream, and John Addis was a hunter from early on in his life, and he loved guns.

On the map, the state is one of the most bizarre-looking land configurations of any in America. It is separated into two parts: the Lower Peninsula and the Upper Peninsula. The Lower Peninsula is a huge, awkward-looking, at times meandering spit of land jutting into two colossal bodies of freshwater—Lake Huron to its east and Lake Michigan to its west. Each lake is a fisherman's paradise, offering bountiful fisheries of steelhead, coho salmon, rainbow trout, perch, and many, many others. Lake Michigan is more than 300 miles long and 118 miles wide at its widest point.

It offers breathtaking scenery of glorious, white sandy beaches, panorama bluffs, and Bermuda-like blue waters from Benton Harbor to Manistee, Traverse City to Mackinaw City. Its little-sister lake, Huron, to its east, is perhaps Michigan's most underrated natural feature. One can drive from Detroit, along the eastern side of the state, through what Michiganders call the "thumb" of the state, and head north, traveling alongside thick, burly pine forests to the left and picturesque lake views of the lovely Huron to the right.

The Lower Peninsula is connected to the Upper Peninsula by the stunning Mackinac Bridge, which stretches a remarkable five miles from Mackinaw City to the gates of the wild Upper Peninsula. Known to Michiganders as the U.P., it is comparable in America to perhaps only one other place—Alaska. It is that wild. The body of land is home to just 3 percent of Michigan's population, but it is very big, stretching from St. Ignace to the Keweenaw Peninsula and eventually to Wisconsin on the way to Northern Minnesota. The Upper Peninsula, as you travel north, is eventually engulfed by the mighty Lake Superior—one of the great natural wonders of America. It is the largest freshwater lake by surface area in the world, and it is an intimidating body of water. It is icy cold, deep, and dark. It is also a lake with its own weather systems because it is so incredibly big, and it is a lake that eats even the most massive freighters when steered by ship captains who don't submit and pay heed to Superior's powers. The crew of the historic freighter *Edmund Fitzgerald* so tragically learned this lesson in its fateful journey and sinking in 1975, but the lake has been doing that to ships and schooners for hundreds of years.

—————————

Addis was born in Flint, Michigan, on September 19, 1950, to John Raymond Addis, originally of Holly, Michigan, and Anita Syrene Peterson, a native of Flint. Not a whole lot about Addis's early life is known or has ever been documented publicly, but he was definitely good-looking from the start. He had blond hair and green eyes, and he was physically strong. He has four sisters. One of his sisters works in an insurance office in the Midwest; another is a very talented artist.

John's family in Southern Michigan declined to comment on behalf of his family for this book. The family is devastated by the pain Addis caused a lot of good people in his life.

It is clear Addis is from a good family. He was born and raised during a time in Southern Michigan that was far different from today. It was a time when the auto industry in Southern Michigan was booming, at the center of the Michigan economy, and John would later tell his co-workers he loved the state of Michigan with all his heart. He was raised to hunt and fish, and he loved the woods. He also told people he'd spent a lot of time in Calumet, Michigan, in the Upper Peninsula's Keweenaw Peninsula and on the cusp of Lake Superior. Addis actually claimed to some that he was born and raised in Calumet, in the U.P., although a passport application filled out by Addis clearly identifies Flint as his birthplace.

Growing up in the Milford area in the 1960s, John Patrick Addis was athletic, good-looking, and a very straitlaced kid. Milford is a suburban area in western Oakland County, Michigan, on the Huron River and featuring nice parks. Addis was very talented as a young man in the world of music. He played the French horn, piano, and guitar, and he seemed perfectly normal to those around him. He was very much an athlete, he had a good personality, he was incredibly intelligent, and he was into physical fitness. Anyone who knew Addis would unfailingly say he was intent on keeping his body and mind in the best shape possible. He did not drink, and he did not do drugs. He ran for miles at a time, did sit-ups almost daily, and lifted weights. He was careful about what he ate, and over time, he expressed an interest in science and perhaps a career as a doctor. He loved to play tennis, and he loved to hunt. He was also, in public settings at least, very proper and formal and respectful.

Addis graduated from high school in Milford and briefly enrolled in college in Michigan to study biology in preparation for a career in medicine. He also worked as a lab technician for a while, and it was in Michigan that Addis met his first wife, Emma Freed.* Emma is a petite woman with dark hair. She is an honorable, hardworking woman trained as a professional nurse. The couple married in Houghton, Michigan, which serves as the gateway to the Keweenaw Peninsula in Upper Michigan. Addis would later claim he went to college at Houghton's Michigan Technological University. After marrying in Houghton, the couple planned to build a family, possibly in Michigan.

3 ... ALASKA STATE TROOPERS

To the lover of wilderness. Alaska is one of the most wonderful countries in the world.

—John Muir

When it came time to pass the classes and prove a long-term commitment to college in Michigan, John Addis suddenly decided that he didn't want to pursue a career in medicine or science anymore. He was rejecting the career path and taking a completely different turn. What he truly enjoyed, he said, was hunting and living the outdoorsman's life. He loved to hunt deer in Michigan in both the Upper Peninsula and Lower Peninsula. He camped a lot, and he was very interested in guns. He loved guns. He particularly loved hunting deer with rifles.

Addis read a lot of hunting magazines, and Alaska appealed to him. He would later tell friends the state seemed to be calling him. He loved the wildness of Michigan's Upper Peninsula, and Alaska was the next and greatest step for a true American outdoorsman. Brown bear, caribou, elk, and moose could be hunted there. The state is huge—much, much bigger than Texas. In fact, it is larger than America's three other largest states combined.

In the early 1970s, Addis announced to his new wife, Emma, that he wanted to move to Alaska and eventually pursue a job in law enforcement. Emma's reaction to the prospect of living in the most sparsely populated and wild state in America is unknown, but what is known is that she would one day view Addis's about-face from attending college to wanting to live in rural Alaska as an indicator of her husband's proclivity for failing and then blaming others for his problems. He was a person who would talk of doing great things, such as going to medical school, but not follow through. He'd had ambitious dreams of medical school. He was incredibly talented and charming. He was brilliant. Many of his friends would later describe him as a "genius" when it came to math and science. But Emma later described how Addis's dreams never seemed to materialize.

"It was always somebody else's fault," Emma would later tell the *Fairbanks Daily News-Miner* newspaper in December 1986. "Either his parents didn't have enough influence or I didn't write the right letter. . . . 'It's my dream, but you guys have to make it come true for me.'"

Law enforcement colleagues and acquaintances of John in Alaska would later describe him as a man of very strong will who was going to do what he wanted to do. Emma was likely along for the ride, they said, even if she didn't want to move to Alaska. The couple first settled in the small city of Sitka, on Baranof Island in southeastern Alaska, where Addis took a job as a local dogcatcher. There are no roads to the city of roughly nine thousand people—you have to fly or arrive by sea there. It is part of the Alexander

Archipelago chain of islands, and Emma found herself a long way from Michigan as she and Addis set about raising a family there.

"I was married to John for almost eleven years," Emma would later tell a Las Vegas grand jury. "We were married in 1971 and divorced in 1982."

Early in the marriage, she saw John as a dream of a man and husband despite their abrupt move to Alaska. Emma also liked that he was rather old-fashioned. He wanted to spend a lot of time with her. He was a man who was meticulous about everything, rigid in his attention to detail, and he had a passion for life, too. He loved being outdoors, and he wanted children. He wanted to be a family man more than anything. Emma gave birth to four children. Their first daughter, Charlotte,* was born in June 1973. A second daughter, Mary Beth,* was born in September 1975. The couple's first son, Richard Franklin,* was born in March 1980. Their fourth child, a daughter, Susan Leigh,* was born in 1981.

Addis's stint patrolling the streets of Sitka for wayward dogs was short-lived. He hired on with the local police force there and then joined the Alaska State Troopers in 1974, a year after his first daughter was born. His first assignment was Fort Yukon, a small city in northern Alaska, where he handled everything from routine public-intoxication calls to investigations in the Alaskan bush. He worked as a state cop in Fort Yukon before transferring to Fairbanks in the mid-1970s. Within a matter of years, Addis would become a bush pilot and outdoorsman of legendary talent in the eyes of many of his colleagues. He also became an incredibly daring bush pilot enchanted with Alaska's mountain ranges. He was particularly fond of the Brooks

Range—often termed the most resplendent in Alaska and within flying distance of his original assignment of Fort Yukon. The natural beauty of the Brooks Range was described by explorer Robert Marshall in *Alaska Wilderness: Exploring the Central Brooks Range*. Marshall's descriptions of life and explorations in the largely pristine Brooks Range for more than a decade remained true for Addis as he flew through the range in his Cessna 185D some four decades after these words about one of Marshall's many adventures in the Brooks were first written:

"It was full starlight when we started, headed straight back on the course toward Polaris," Marshall wrote of one exploration through the mountain wilderness. "After half an hour the black sky began to turn gray, and the Arctic brightness of the stars slowly faded. The gray became faintly blue, and then a single snowy peak in the northwest showed a tip of pink. . . . The pink spread from peak to peak . . . [and then] vanished, and you noticed the mountainsides were bathed in a golden spray—craggy peaks, snowfields, dark spruce, everything."

This is the type of scenery John Addis would adore while in Alaska. He sought it out regularly, flying into the bush and the mountains in his plane or landing on a riverbank and spending days at a time camping. The bush and the mountains of Alaska, arresting and transcendent in their pure beauty, were the places where Addis sought peace.

Addis's hiring on with the Alaska State Troopers in 1974 put him on the payroll of a very unique law enforcement organization. The agency is where Addis learned to be a hard-nosed cop responsible for enforcing the law for much of the 1970s.

The state troopers in Alaska face very unique obstacles in keeping the peace. The agency is known as an excellent policing operation responsible for covering 586,000 square miles of territory. The agency, on its website, calls itself the "First Response in the Last Frontier" and says it keeps the peace despite "blizzards, hundreds of inches of snowfall, avalanches, winds in excess of one hundred miles per hour, sub-zero temperatures, and heavy rainfall. The state is filled with rugged mountains, massive glaciers, tundra, forests, more than three thousand rivers, more than three million lakes and a coastline of six thousand six hundred and forty miles."

Today, the troopers have two hundred and forty officers and nearly that many civilian employees. The officers are described as the "blue shirts," who patrol the cities and the towns, and the "brown shirts," who enforce wildlife rules. The headquarters for the troopers is in Anchorage, and there are outposts, or detachments, throughout the state. Some of those outposts are very remote and subjected to the most extreme weather conditions. The citizenry of Alaska is also heavily armed, and policing calls can take troopers into the bush for days, sometimes by themselves. There is little backup for the state police in Alaska. If there is backup, it is often hours away, meaning troopers have to be completely self-sufficient in the field and also extremely cautious because there most likely won't be anyone to help if things go badly. The diverse geographic challenges the agency faces require the state troopers to have an assorted set of tools in their arsenal. The state troopers have aircraft

and marine units that feature airplanes, helicopters, snow-
mobiles, all-terrain vehicles, and boats. The agency relies
on a cadre of troopers capable of handling the toughest
assignments. They have to handle the traditional calls—
the domestic-violence incidents, the drunks, and traffic
issues—but at least some of the troopers also have to be
able to fly a plane into the bush and land it in fields, putting
their lives at risk so Alaskan families can enjoy a peaceful
quality of life with protection from the law.

One of the most recognized figures in Alaska law
enforcement's modern era is James "Jim" McCann—a
retired sergeant and homicide investigator with the Alaska
State Troopers. He gave his sweat and blood and time to
the agency for twenty-eight years. He is an old-school cop
and a hard-charging investigator. He is a man known to
speak his mind and tell you what he thinks. He was, for
decades, a media darling in state police investigation. He
was in the newspaper constantly while investigating the
area's major homicide cases with his fellow detectives at
the Fairbanks, Alaska, post.

He worked with fellow trooper John Patrick Addis at
the Fairbanks detachment for years, and he came to know
Addis very well. The two became very good friends.

"I knew him to be a very conservative man," McCann
said.

Tough and *strong* are the first words that come to mind
when McCann thinks of Addis. "Jar-faced. Chiseled fea-
tures—his face was very chiseled."

McCann, sixty, is a man who, like Addis, pays attention to fitness and keeps himself in good shape. McCann,
at six feet three, likes to hunt. Now retired, he can't envi-
sion himself living anywhere other than Alaska. He is an

expert sportsman who enjoys going into the outdoors with his dogs and hunting for quail, ruffed grouse, sharp-tailed grouse, and other game.

"I'm a hunter," McCann said. "I've been working for outdoor magazines, and I've got one book [*Upland Hunting in Alaska: The Bird Hunter's Guide*]. I've probably written more about fly-fishing. I guess it's because I had to get into something other than murder."

McCann was born and raised in New York State—Ossining—on the Hudson, just up from Tarrytown and above Yonkers but below West Point. McCann's dad was an Irish cop, Charles McCann, or "Charlie," who strolled the streets in Bronxville. McCann has one brother, Charles Jr.

"I walked the beat with my dad, watched him twirl the baton and talk with people on the street," McCann said.

"I guess my dad being a cop gave me the idea. I nurtured it over time, and all of my own heroes in life were all cops," McCann said. "You know the old clichés—'I want to get the job done and I want to help people and catch bad guys.' Well, that's really true. I want to help good people and kick ass."

McCann's wife, Gail, is a lovely woman. She's five feet seven inches tall, with a slight build and lighter hair that was once dark. She has blue eyes and is an artist. She said she met her future husband in high school in Ossining. She respected him immediately and loves Jim dearly.

"He was always a hunter," Gail says of her husband. "His father was in law enforcement and wasn't home a lot, so my dad took Jim hunting and fishing."

He was handsome, honest, and loved her right away.

"He is a man of integrity," Gail says of her husband. "I admire him to this day. He's a man of honor."

"She loves me," Jim McCann responds. "We are good friends, too."

Jim McCann, like John Addis, was a man raised to hunt, and he, too, dreamed of going to Alaska one day. He'd talked about it since he was a very young man.

"My dreams always went straight to Alaska," Jim McCann said. "I'd read about it and dreamed about it for years. For deer hunting, I could only afford one rifle, so I bought a Winchester Model 70 in .338 magnum. A bigger gun, but I knew I was going to Alaska one day, so I was thinking ahead."

Jim McCann first met John Addis when they were stationed together at the state trooper barracks in Fairbanks. The city, in a large valley, is home to some ninety thousand people and is commonly referred to as the end of the Alaska highway. It is a place where the summer days are very long and the winters are even longer, bringing with them occasional glimpses of the aurora borealis, skiing, snowboarding, and snowmobiling. Life in Fairbanks can be as suburban as you want it to be or, if you drive out of town just a little bit, as remote as you want it to be. Life in this city, as described by Jim McCann, is completely normal.

"Fairbanks is like any other city in the United States," McCann said. "It doesn't have igloos, and we don't all live in cabins."

Yet John Patrick Addis—when he moved to Fairbanks—seemed intent on having his family live the life lived by men and women in Alaska one hundred years earlier. Addis wanted the frontier life. He wanted the life in a cabin, and he set about living that way whether his family liked it or not. He moved his wife, Emma, and their children to a tiny one-room cabin outside of Fairbanks. The home had no running water. They heated the tiny home with wood, and Addis refused to hook up his home to the electric grid. When he needed power, he used a generator. The Addis home was very rural. It was located in the Goldstream Valley and the nearby White Mountains area. The area is known for black bear and other wildlife, and Addis's home was situated in a place where, at least in the 1970s, packs of rabid wolves stalked sled dogs and family pooches for an entire winter.

Addis bought eighty acres in the Goldstream, and he made it clear to everyone he wanted it to be remote. Emma, meanwhile, was a registered nurse, but John wanted her staying home with the children.

"He was different than the rest of us," James McCann said. "His wife, Emma, gave him his haircuts. It was Alaska, the 'Last Frontier,' but still, John was different than everyone else. Everyone was tough, but he was the one who really wanted to live in a cabin out in the woods."

Just driving to Addis's home was an adventure every rainy spring. The bumpy, muddy road grinded the bottom of his buddies' patrol cars. Addis often had to park his patrol car halfway down the road because of the mud.

"His driveway, [it] was often [necessary to have a] four-wheel drive. It was often muddy in the spring. . . . He had a four-wheel-drive truck at the time, and he would bounce his way into his place."

Addis's co-workers at the state troopers quickly took notice that John was very consumed by living the rural, remote lifestyle. He was also quirky, by uptight state cop standards. At times it seemed like he'd just emerged from the woods with little preparation for cleanliness and the pressing of his uniform.

"John was also a little bit different than the rest of [the troopers], who were always trying to keep uniforms absolutely perfect, shoes shined. Perfect and pressed," McCann said. "John was a little unkempt, and he smelled of wood all the time."

"He dressed casually [a lot]," McCann said. "As a matter of fact, he was the kind of police officer that would wear his police shoes with Levis after work. I mean, something everybody else would look at and say, 'Gee.' He was an outdoorsman. He was a hunter, fisherman. More a hunter than a fisherman. He loved firearms. He had a large collection of firearms, handguns, rifles, shotguns, all varieties. He was very knowledgeable in the use of firearms and ammunition and the components."

For some reason, it seemed to Jim McCann that Addis was running from something in life. Trying to get away into the woods.

"It was basically the lure of the woods for him, and I always got the sense he may have displeased his parents by saying he was going to go to medical school and then giving that up," McCann said.

Gail McCann was struck by the lifestyle the Addis family was living when she first visited their cabin in the Goldstream. Namely, she was struck by how small it was. John and Emma had just two daughters at the time of the McCanns' first visit. Gail McCann was amazed that all four lived in the small cabin with no running water and only a woodstove. Some witnesses said it only had a dirt floor—it was pioneer living to the extreme. Gail recognized that with no running water, no washer and dryer, no dishwasher, and electricity provided only by a generator, her friend Emma must lead a very difficult existence. The woman had to wash clothes in a tub. She had to haul water when it was bitterly cold out. You couldn't just take a hot shower. The water had to be heated. You couldn't just get up and walk to the bathroom in the middle of the night. You had to go outside to the outhouse.

"The cabin was little—as big as a bedroom," Jim McCann recalled. "Everyone thought, 'John, geez, you have your wife and two kids in this little place?' No plumbing. Outhouse. It was all pretty awkward."

"That was John," Gail recalled, adding the cabin was "a ways from town. He was kind of farming. He had sheep or goats or something. It was great fun to go out there with the kids. At the time, he had two girls, and I think she was expecting the first boy."

The Addis and McCann families were friends because of John and Jim's time together at the Fairbanks office of the Alaska State Troopers, and they spent time together on weekends. Paul Bartlett, a longtime pilot for the Alaska state police, got to be very good friends with Addis and visited the Addis family at their rural home in the Goldstream. He, too, found the living conditions a little extreme, "but that was John."

"When I hired on [with the state troopers] in Fairbanks, John was stationed at Fort Yukon and then John transferred from Fort Yukon into Fairbanks, and I found him to be very outgoing and very much a sportsman," Bartlett said. "John and I hunted together, and we went on several hunts together. We got to be good friends working patrol in Fairbanks. I got to know his family—his wife, Emma, and the girls, and then his son—and I used to visit them quite a bit."

Roger McCoy, another state trooper who spent much of his career in Fairbanks, described the frontier living conditions at the Addis home as extreme.

"He [Addis] did a good job and he was very good at what he did, but he had some weird ideas," McCoy said. "For his wife and children, he insisted they live in a cabin that had no floor. It was just the ground. There was no electricity and you had to go outside, to the outhouse, because there was no bathroom inside. He had a generator but he would not hook up to the local power line."

McCoy, sixty-seven, spent nearly three decades as an Alaska trooper, regularly doing investigations in the bush, in Eskimo villages, or in the urban areas of Fairbanks and Anchorage. He is a very nice, courteous man who has seen the darker side of human existence through his work in law enforcement. He became a lead major investigator in the second and fourth districts of Alaska State Trooper jurisdiction, including Fairbanks and the Alaskan North Slope. McCoy got to be close friends with fellow trooper John Patrick Addis. McCoy, in fact, was related by marriage to Addis, through Addis's wife, Emma, who was McCoy's sister-in-law. McCoy described Addis as a truly talented investigator.

"He was about six feet one, two hundred pounds, and, really, a good-looking guy," McCoy said. "A really handsome guy. He was highly intelligent. Very tenacious and highly, highly intelligent. An excellent investigator. He was very thorough and an expert in just about everything."

He described Addis's refusal to get electricity as what he suspects was Addis's commitment to never rely on the government for anything. Although Addis worked for the state, he did not trust the government. Addis seemed at the time to be wary of authority and wanted to be completely self-reliant.

"It's the way he lived, and [his wife and kids] just had to go along with it," McCoy said.

Gail McCann said that despite the living conditions, the families of Addis's colleagues at the state trooper barracks did not judge Addis and Emma. They figured they wanted to live out in the country, and Gail McCann said all of the state trooper families "could let our hair down in front of one another." The families used to go on picnics, and many of the wives became good friends. She at first saw nothing wrong with John Addis other than the remoteness of his lifestyle and the quirkiness that came along with it.

"John Addis was very prudish," Gail said. "You didn't make sexual jokes or anything like that. A very straitlaced man."

Gail McCann knew John as a musician as well. He told her he'd played in an orchestra or band in high school and also at college in Michigan briefly. She remembered him as being very talented in this regard.

"He told me he was a premed student, and he gave my husband a clarinet or coronet," Gail McCann said. "He played, like, a trumpet. He had a recording of an orchestra at some school in Michigan, some college, where he played, and he was involved there at a college level in orchestra.

"Just kind of a straitlaced guy," Gail McCann said. "You don't talk about things that are not proper. 'We have women and kids here.'"

Gail McCann distinctly remembers going to dinner evenings at the Addis home in the woods.

"A couple of times, we went to their home for dinner," Gail said. "We went out there with our families, and it was pleasant, but I would always leave thinking I would not want to live like that. They would haul their own water, probably from a spring in Fairbanks where a lot of people fill up their jugs.

"They had an outhouse," Gail McCann said. "It was hard for her, Emma. She had little kids, she was pregnant, and they were all preschoolers.

"We always thought John should have been born a century earlier," Gail McCann said. "A pioneer guy."

4 ... CRIME SCENES

John Addis's co-workers in Fairbanks quickly concluded he was a very sharp cop. Within two years of working as a lowly dogcatcher in Sitka, he was noticed for his very strong work ethic and his fastidious attention to detail. He was a straitlaced, conservative patrol cop in a world of political controversy, the 1960s revolution continuing into the 1970s, Vietnam, and Watergate. His supervisors thought he had the potential to be a truly excellent law enforcement officer with unlimited potential to rise up through the ranks and be a skilled investigator.

Addis was also mildly popular in the state trooper barracks and was responsible for getting most of his Fairbanks co-workers interested in physical fitness. McCann spent a lot of time lifting weights and jogging with Addis at the state trooper post in Fairbanks. Addis was known for bench-pressing a lot of weight for his size.

"John got me started lifting weights," Jim McCann said.

Paul Bartlett was impressed with John's strength on the weight bench as well.

"Very strong," Bartlett said. "He worked out a lot, and I remember him pressing every bit of weight that was available on this big gym machine at the Fairbanks post. It still wasn't enough, so he put one of his kids on top of the weights, and he was very strong. He pressed that, too."

One of John's passions that continued in the state troopers was rifles. He was an excellent sharpshooter. He told his colleagues that he was taught how to be a shooter growing up in Michigan. He spent a lot of time practicing his marksmanship. Doing so requires great patience and knowledge about guns, and Addis could put a bullet in a precise target from hundreds of yards away. This skill would come in handy when Addis and Jim McCann helped get a SWAT team started in the Alaska Troopers.

"He was one of the original five members of the state SWAT team," McCann said. "Some place I've got pictures of me and John . . . when we helped with protection for President Ford when he came here. We were pretty new to stuff, new techniques in law enforcement, and we modified everything to be the best we could be. We also worked out together, to get tougher, and [we] really worked out a lot."

Addis worked patrol and SWAT, but Jim McCann said John Addis's specialty at the Alaska State Troopers' Fairbanks detachment was crime-scene investigation. Addis was very good at it. Addis wasn't necessarily the best interviewer of suspects, but the man could process a crime scene. He had a scientific and math-based mind. There was no state crime lab at the time, and McCann said he and Addis became a sort of self-sustaining crime lab out of the Fairbanks unit.

"We got to know each other," Jim McCann said. "He professed to be a medical student, almost a doctor, and said he did have a biology background. Well, the Alaska State Troopers was a pretty small group, and someone with [a] college [background like him] kind of stood out."

Addis, Jim McCann said, "had the ability to get you all excited about forensics."

McCann himself was once described by Alaskan author Tom Brennan in his popular book *Murder at 40 Below: True Crime Stories from Alaska* as "one of the most capable, dedicated, and creative homicide detectives to ever work in Alaska," and McCann credits Addis with developing forensics and the latest techniques for police protocol in major homicide investigations. McCann, with the help of some of the techniques he learned from Addis, was responsible for investigating some of Alaska's biggest cases, including the rape and murder of college student Sophie Sergei at the University of Alaska at Fairbanks. The sexual homicide occurred in a women's bathroom on campus and remains unsolved. McCann was a critical part of the investigation into serial killer Thomas Richard Bunday, who terrorized portions of Alaska by killing five young women in and around 1980. He committed suicide by driving his motorcycle in front of a car in Texas. Bunday is ranked second in Alaska criminal history as one of the state's most dangerous and frightening men, submitting only to the extreme cruelty of killer Robert Hansen. Hansen's claim to fame was his macabre sport of flying women out into the wilderness and then hunting them for sport.

McCann was also a lead investigator in a murder case that captivated all of Alaska and, later, the nation. The homicide involved Alaskan Independence Party founder

Joe Vogler. Vogler, a native of Kansas, moved to Alaska and was well-known in the Fairbanks area as a miner who had a rebellious streak. Vogler repeatedly ran for governor in the state and advocated for Alaska to secede.

"I'm an Alaskan, not an American," Vogler was once quoted as saying. "I've got no use for America or her damned institutions."

Vogler disappeared in May 1993. McCann worked the investigation and turned up a shallow grave containing Vogler's eighty-year-old body. The murder was tied to a common thief in the area and was eventually featured on the television show *American Justice*.

"On homicides, I would always keep a photo of the victim with me at my desk," McCann said. "I'd have a nice photo of the victim, an eight by ten or whatever I could get, and I'd keep it right there on my desk, and keep it near me. I would look at that picture, and it would keep me saying, 'Let's get going,' because I represented them."

Addis, McCann said, was an expert on forensic-science techniques and the gathering of evidence for the specific purpose of criminal prosecution. The two men were constantly reading and taking college classes to boost the prowess of their homemade forensics unit. They investigated, and at the same time, they did their own scientific collection of evidence. There was no roaming crime lab in those days in Alaska. The men did their own dusting for prints and took their own photographs.

Addis was an expert on the collection of fiber evidence. He practiced time and again the method of bagging evidence, returning the item to the police station, and using combs and microscopes to look for hairs that could help include or exclude a suspect as being at the scene of a

crime. He knew the particulars of collecting hair samples
from individuals for comparison to hairs collected from
crime scenes. Addis performed extensive studies on the
ability to recover synthetic fibers from items of evidence or
bodies and compare them to carpet samples.

Addis was very wise to the various techniques that help
police search for biological clues. He studied blood spray
patterns and the best ways to retrieve blood samples from
evidence for examination of blood types. He studied blood
blowback patterns from the discharge of a firearm into a
human body. He could examine patterns from shotgun
stippling and make close estimates as to how far away the
weapon was from a body when it was fired. He was an
expert on the various stages of decomposition, which can
indicate to an investigator a time of death for the deceased.
Addis also earned a reputation as an expert on the study
of insect life and how it impacts decomposition. Addis
knew that certain types of flies and bugs were attracted to
the human body after death, and he could help authorities
determine a time of death for the deceased by looking at
what insects were on human remains when discovered.

"If he had a specialty, it was definitely [processing] the
crime scenes," Jim McCann said. "Dealing with people
and that sort of stuff—people liked him—but he was very
rigid, and he wasn't a people person as much as he was the
scientist.

"He understood it, and that's what we talked about with
him a lot," McCann said. "We learned whatever techniques
we could. I'm not a scientific guy, and John spurred that
on in me. Learning things and discussing how we did our
crime-scene investigation.

"To do [photos], we needed 35 mm slides, so we just

did it," Jim McCann said. "We bought our own slides [and] film. There was no money for processing, so we'd get our own processing kit and do it ourselves. We'd do it right there in the bathroom, in the [state troopers' office in Fairbanks]. This was prepipeline days when you made a thousand dollars a month, but we processed our own slides, evidence, fingerprints, fluids, gunshot evidence. You name it. We did all of that stuff."

Addis was simultaneously making a lot of contacts with professors at the University of Alaska at Fairbanks. He was constantly reaching out to professors to learn more about science and how it could be applied to catching criminals in the Fairbanks area. He was a student of the art of forensics. He studied everything from serology to lifting prints off the most obscure and roughly surfaced objects. He used his lab-technician background to perform blood tests and other examinations under the microscope.

"We started to pal around a little bit with forensic pathologists, and in 1976 or '77, John and I did pretty much the first death homicide investigation [seminar] in Alaska," Jim McCann said. "We had defense attorneys talk, prosecutors talk, and pathologists. It was a three-day seminar, and it was very well accepted."

Jim McCann said John Addis understood a lot about crime scenes. He knew all about how police collected clues.

He'd done it himself.

"He and I [even taught] a lot of crime-scene investigation classes," he said. "As far as crime scenes go, he was very good. He was not that good at dealing with people, so as an overall successful investigator, I would not consider him a successful investigator, but if you gave him a crime scene to work to gather evidence, to identify evidence, to properly handle that evidence, and then transmit that evidence to a laboratory, to know what you can get as evidence and to be aware of the science and the technology that's out there, well, John Addis knew it."

In many ways, Addis was boosting his stock as a state trooper through his knowledge of forensics. It wasn't always an area of expertise state troopers gravitated to, but Addis appreciated very deeply how valuable science could be in catching killers and locking up bad guys.

"Without a crime scene, you have no case, but John was good at finding evidence," McCann said. "I don't say that lightly. I don't take that lightly. I find a crime scene is very important and usually like to do them myself or to be there at every crime scene, but John Addis, back then, if he were available to do a crime scene, I would let John Addis do my crime scene with me. He was that thorough and knowledgeable. I might also add that he had a lot of contact with the professors at the university and convinced them to start to develop a forensic-science curriculum of which I had taken some of those classes also. I remember one in particular was forensic anthropology. John was very instrumental in developing that curriculum.

"But in conversing with people and trying to get information from people, you know . . . [Addis] was very conservative," McCann said.

5 . . . BUSH PILOT

John Addis seemed to have everything going for him in the mid-1970s. He was on the payroll of the Alaska State Troopers, and, although he was never going to get rich working in policing, he could live in Alaska, hunt, and be pretty much guaranteed he would get a retirement package when he hung up the badge. He was becoming very well recognized as the Fairbanks bureau's most knowledgeable forensics expert, and he hung out at the barracks a lot, lifting weights with his buddies and going jogging. He was a big, strong, strapping state cop who was known for working hard and giving the day his most diligent effort. He had a beautiful wife and family—two kids (and going on three) by the late 1970s—and he loved living in the rural Goldstream Valley of Alaska. He found peace being among the towering pines and looking up, watching them sway back and forth, in the chilled, powerful Alaska winds. He loved the surrounding mountains, the beautiful open valley of the Goldstream, and the area's luxuriant trails for skiers, mushers, snowmobilers, and bikers.

Addis, in 1981, announced to his fellow state troopers he was going to build a new cabin on the land that housed the small cabin he, his wife, and his three children were already living in. The new cabin would be bigger. He was going to cut the trees, remove the bark, and stack the trees all by himself. The idea of Addis building an entire log home by hand, largely by himself, was typical John. He was an outdoorsman to the core.

Jim McCann was invited to help out.

"He got a permit to cut logs and went out and did his own logging," McCann said. "I helped him do that. We worked our asses off hauling logs."

The building of the cabin was a family affair for Addis. Emma and the couple's daughters helped skin the logs with McCann. Everyone was expected to help out and not ask questions. John directed them on what to do.

"Sometimes I would go along with him, we would go out and cut down trees and trim them, and he would bring them back to his property, where he and his wife and daughters would peel them, and [they] actually built a much larger home," McCann said. "Still a much more rural setting.

"Emma didn't talk too much," McCann added.

Fellow state trooper Paul Bartlett was asked by Addis to help with the new cabin, too.

"It was a remote cabin in the Goldstream Valley—all natural logs," Bartlett said. "It was pretty rough, but he was able to heat it with just wood."

Bartlett said he was impressed with Addis as a man. He was a tough survivalist and a big, strong man who could handle a chain saw like a master. He was an expert woodsman and marksman. He was very good with a knife. He was a hard worker, he was a smart cop, and Bartlett considered Addis a dear friend.

"For the longest time, I thought he was the greatest guy," Bartlett said.

Bartlett, sixty-six, was born in Bridgeport, Connecticut. He is a soft-spoken, clean-shaven, gray-haired man with a set of green eyes that have witnessed great expanses of terrain from the air in Vietnam and Alaska. He flies both helicopters and fixed-wing aircraft. He moved to New Hampshire with his family as a child, and he had a brother who lived in Fairbanks, so Bartlett visited Alaska as a young man and was taken by its beauty. He got a draft notice in 1968 and enlisted in the U.S. Army. Bartlett eventually went to flight school and flew helicopters in Vietnam, direct commission. After returning from the combat zone, he was stationed at the Fort Wainwright army base in Alaska. Bartlett then joined the Alaska State Troopers and "spent ten years in the bush," policing at stations in Bethel, Nome, and Antioch. He operated autonomously for much of his lengthy state trooper career, often using his plane to swoop in and out of the bush, all in the name of justice and caring for his fellow citizen. He became good friends with Addis and took him up in his plane regularly.

Bartlett said that over time Addis expressed an interest in being a pilot like Bartlett. He and Addis flew into the wilderness often in Bartlett's plane, and Addis was constantly seeking out advice and tips on how to be a pilot. Bartlett could tell Addis wanted to be a pilot, too. Addis started taking private flying lessons regularly in Fairbanks. He slowly learned how to be a bush pilot, and it helped that Bartlett and McCann—his fellow troopers—were bush pilots, too.

"I gave him a lot of tips on flying," Bartlett said. "During the time we knew each other, he was getting his private pilot's license, and then he decided he was going to buy an Aeronca Sedan."

The aircraft is a small four-seater perfect for flying into the wilderness and landing in small spots. As Addis flew more and more, it became apparent to his colleagues that he was becoming a very good pilot. He was described as a very daring aviator willing to land his plane on a glacier or in the smallest of fields and openings in the woods. He often landed his plane in a grassy area near his cabin. He also was known to go flying with his daughters, taking them into the wilderness for an afternoon in the bush. Addis's piloting skills improved, and he eventually graduated from the Aeronca to flying Cessnas.

"He was always flying off with his daughters," McCann said, adding Addis was definitely "a bush pilot. There was a little grass strip up where he lived that he landed his [plane at his] place. We'd fly up into the Alaska Range and Brooks Range mountains."

Fellow trooper Roger McCoy described Addis as daring to the extreme while flying. The man was not afraid of taking risks that could feasibly cause him to crash. He flew in bad weather, and he rarely, if ever, filed a flight plan. Most pilots would never think of taking such risks. Addis, however, seemed to revel in his fearlessness. He felt that if he crashed and wasn't badly injured, he would survive, particularly if it was summertime. Addis was also knowledgeable about building snow caves, staying warm, and finding food from the land even in the dead of winter. He always carried a large hunting knife with him just in case.

"John was very adventurous, and he would get in his

plane, and he would just go fly away without any planning whatsoever," McCoy said. "You are supposed to do a flight plan wherever you go, especially in Alaska, but he didn't want to rely on the government in any way. He didn't trust people."

They flew repeatedly into the pure Alaska wilderness, with its snowcapped mountains, its hugely rolling rivers with their whitecaps and salmon runs, and its grassy pastures and wild lands, and they hunted. They tracked down Alaska's great hunting targets—moose and deer—and Bartlett came to conclude that Addis was a rare breed: a man who could literally live in the wild with nothing if he had to.

"You have to understand what John was like. . . . John was very smart," Bartlett said. "Very smart. He trained to the tenth degree in whatever he did. He could survive out there [in the wilderness]. You could turn him loose with a gun and knife, and he'd be able to make it. That's what John was like."

One of Bartlett's most interesting accounts of his friendship with Addis unfolded in September 1981. That month, Bartlett was assigned to pick up a trooper in Fort Yukon by aircraft. He took off in a state troopers' Cessna 207, and while in the air, he scouted the Porcupine River as a potential hunting spot for him and his buddies. The state troopers also wanted him to perform a welfare check during the flight to Fort Yukon on a man who was reported to be camping at an unknown and unnamed lake somewhere northwest of the intersection of the Colleen River and the Porcupine River. The man was Carl McCunn. He'd been flown into the remote lake in March 1981 without making arrangements for his return. Bartlett flew over the man's camp, and McCunn waved back with one arm in the air.

"Carl emerged from his tent waving his hand," Bartlett said. "He displayed no distress and didn't signal a need for rescue, which would be both hands held above his head. I circled the lake about four times, assumed he was fine, then proceeded to the Porcupine River, checking the moose population, while flying to Old Crow."

Bartlett said while scouting the hunting trip in Old Crow, "The Mounties met us and provided us a tour of the village and a steak and lobster dinner with an overnight stay." In the spring of 1982, Bartlett would learn, however, that McCunn had confused his rescue signals. Two hands in the air meant he needed help. One hand meant he was fine.

"The person who asked for the welfare check was given the information, and nothing more was done until February 1982, when his body was found in his tent with a fatal gunshot wound," Bartlett said. "He elected to take his life rather than starve. The better option would have been walking to the Colleen River a short distance to the east. That time of year moose hunters invade that area by boat. Carl McCunn wrote in his diary about the day I flew over thinking he was about to be rescued. Some months later he thought to look at his Alaskan hunting license and found he gave the signal that he was OK and needed no assistance."

Two days after the fatal miscommunication with McCunn, Bartlett carried out the hunting trip to the Porcupine River in an adventure that would teach him a lot about what kind of man Addis was. The two went on multiple hunting trips together, facing the bitter cold of the Alaskan wilderness to hunt moose, elk, deer, and bird. The trip on September 12, 1981, entailed Addis flying Bartlett and Sergeant Timothy Litera northeast to the Porcupine River at the Canadian border in Addis's recently purchased Cessna 185D. Addis would drop the men off, and Bartlett and Litera planned a "float hunt" for moose down the wild, tumbling Alaskan river. The men loaded a large inflatable raft in the plane along with their food, guns, and gear and headed out. After flying for a couple of hours, Addis spotted what looked like a gravel landing spot on the river, but the touchdown was rough, and the landing popped a tire on the tail wheel.

"John and Tim unloaded the bulging 185 onto the rock landing strip as I calculated how to fix the tire," Bartlett said. "The tail of the plane was lifted to get the tire off the ground, and I removed the tire with our limited tool supply. The thought of filling the tire with sand came and went. I decided on cutting branches of willows . . . and the tire's internal cavity was packed with small-diameter, thin branches about a foot long that conformed easily."

Addis took off into the air and headed back to Fairbanks with a tire filled with willows and a plan to return seven days later to the mouth of the Colleen River to pick up the men.

"The sound of the 300 horsepower Continental engine faded into the distance," Bartlett said. "The silence of the wilderness is what we heard in minutes."

Bartlett penned the following account of the trip at the request of the author, and he detailed Addis's harrowing flight through a blizzard to pick up the men as they were running out of food:

Tim and I assembled the twelve-foot raft, inflating it and installing the rowing rack in preparation for launch. Our supplies were loaded. Our float trip in this pristine wilderness began. The waters of the river ran swift, clean, and clear, missing the debris of spring run-off. The tree leaves had turned bright yellow as cooler weather was upon us. The smell in the air is profound with the decaying rose hips having its distinctive odor filling the air. The plan was to float an unspecified distance each day and hunt along the way for a moose at the water's edge and camp at different locations each afternoon. On the trip to the Colleen, we saw only a few riverboats with hunters like ourselves.

Arriving at the Colleen River mouth in four days without seeing a moose, we established a camp, putting up a plastic cover over our tent, providing additional protection from the frost and possibility of snow. We hunted the area with no luck. Just being in this spot on earth was reward enough.

The men were running low on food by the fourth day of the trip. A passing boat with moose hunters stopped at their camp and gave them sustenance—extra potatoes, carrots, and onions. The weather was turning bad. It was cold and snowing, and with little food, the men were starting to worry. John was late to pick them up, and they figured it was the weather causing the delay.

We awoke the following morning with six inches of the white stuff on the ground and our shelter over the tent sagging. The first order of business was cutting spruce bows [sic] to mark out a runway on the sand bar beside the Porcupine River in case John showed up in the 185 to take us to Fairbanks. We ate the last of our regular food supplies. Tim bagged a rabbit the previous day.

I prepared to make rabbit stew for the following day. I had a green smoke grenade with me for survival, and it was getting to be that. The grenade was positioned out near the edge of the trees by the runway for quick response when John few [*sic*] by.

The next day brought light snow falling. I prepared the stew; as it was just about done, the drone of an aircraft engine was heard in the distance. We have been hearing the same sound in our minds for several days with nothing being there. There was no mistaking the roar of the 300 horsepower engine now. I ran to the smoke grenade, popping it as John flew past the end of the makeshift runway. It was clear he didn't see it. As the smoke billowed forth and John was disappearing in the light snow flurries, I saw him make a sharp right turn, and that told me he spotted the smoke. Making several passes over the area, he eyed the runway markings, landing on . . . the six-inch carpet of snow. The landing area was significantly different than the drop-off one. As John taxied in Tim and I frantically broke camp packing like most men do, throwing things in helter-skelter. Nearing a panic, we moved rapidly in all that we did. I didn't want to dump the stew, which I cooked in a cleaned-out five-gallon tin fuel can. The stew and all our supplies and raft were quickly loaded in the plane, as the weather wasn't getting any better. John said it was more improved toward Fairbanks, our desti- nation. John, with us and all our supplies, prepared for takeoff . . . [and he flew] his way thru the snow squalls to the clearer skies closer to Fairbanks. John filled us in on the weather situation during our return flight. He had actually . . . flown to Fort Yukon the previous day,

but had to return to Fairbanks due to low ceilings and
poor visibility up the Yukon River. We landed back in
Fairbanks and, looking back, we were thankful to John
for providing us with a memorable life experience.

The men bonded during these outings, and Addis
opened up to his close friend every now and then. On
another hunting trip into the woods, Addis said something
to Bartlett that took the veteran state trooper by surprise.
Addis told Bartlett he saw "little people everywhere."

"He called them 'the thems,'" said Bartlett, who didn't
know quite what to make of the bizarre revelation.

"He was serious," Bartlett said. "[He said] he could see
these little people and he called them 'the thems.' That's
what he called them. . . . I learned later that [this was
something from his] childhood on. He was serious when
he said it."

Bartlett wrote the episode off as a bizarre little quirk.
Perhaps it was a joke. Maybe Addis wasn't really serious,
although he seemed to be serious about believing that there
were little people, invisible to everyone else, everywhere. It
was a bizarre moment, but in the coming years, there would
be many more bizarre events—many strange incidents—
leaving Bartlett questioning whether he ever really knew
his fellow trooper.

"What happened over the next fifteen years or so blew
me away completely," Bartlett would later say. "John was
a good friend, and he is a man who went absolutely crazy."

6 . . . COMPLETE CONTROL

John Addis was observed by his friends to be a very caring father. His friends said the children were everything to John. He spent a lot of time with them. In fact, a lot of his colleagues would later say he took the kids everywhere. When he was off duty from the Alaska State Troopers, he was rarely seen without his wife and children. He particularly spent a lot of time with his daughters.

"A doting father," Gail McCann once observed. "I admired him for it. He loved his kids—the sun rose and set on them."

But although the family looked normal from a distance, behind the scenes, there were problems in the Addis home, and Emma had been keeping a secret throughout the couple's entire marriage. She would later say John became very controlling after the couple moved to Alaska. He could become frightening when no one else was around. The scary side of John was never immediately visible to the outside world, she would later tell friends. The John who frightened her was only observed by those closest to him, and this side of the man only surfaced behind closed doors.

The secret was kept within the family, and for years, John Addis's co-workers attributed John's unique qualities of living a remote lifestyle with no running water and his confession to seeing little humans he called "the thems" to quirkiness. He was definitely a little different, but over time, John Addis's friends began to conclude that maybe it wasn't just quirkiness. Perhaps something wasn't right with their fellow state trooper. Those moments started to unfold in the early 1980s, and they started with a string of events centered around the trooper's treatment of his wife. His friends at the state trooper detachment in Fairbanks noticed that, slowly, Addis was demonstrating some obviously controlling behavior over Emma.

The incidents were subtle at first.

One such episode for Jim McCann unfolded when he noticed Addis calling his wife "mother," as if Emma were his mother—not his wife—but Addis was commanding her around as if he were her boss. Addis, McCann said, ordered her around when he used this term. McCann said he didn't think about it much at the time other than that it was a little strange.

"I remember sitting in his living room, we were talking about guns, and I asked him about a certain type of rifle," McCann said. "He said, 'Oh, I've got one,' and instead of getting up and going and getting it, he said [to Emma], 'Mother, go get me this gun.'"

McCann said Emma returned with the firearm, and he thought the two were probably joking. The gun wasn't the one Addis wanted. Addis expressed his displeasure to his wife, calling her "mother" again, and McCann thought they must be joking.

"So I cracked some smart-ass remark, like, 'Yeah, and mother, bring me a beer!'" McCann recalled.

John glared at his friend. It was clear to McCann at this point that Addis was serious. He actually called his wife "mother."

"John just kind of looked at me, displeased," McCann said. "He looked at me, but he never said anything."

Gail McCann had always thought it was strange that the Addis family lived in such a small home out in the sticks of Alaska, but she never saw abusive behavior by John toward Emma.

"I can remember [after John's] first son was born, John was very supportive of the children," Gail McCann said. "John loved babies, and he seemed to love his own children."

She said the Addis family briefly moved into downtown Fairbanks from the woods, and she and her husband were surprised to see John, all of a sudden, living the city life.

"At that point I didn't spend a lot of time with them once they moved into the new home," Gail McCann said. "Once they moved into their house in downtown Fairbanks, they were there for awhile and then they had their fourth child, and then it wasn't too long after that that the bottom fell out."

Gail McCann would learn years later that John Addis was abusing his wife badly behind closed doors. He verbally abused her, slapped her, choked her, and roughed her up. She would later talk to Emma about the abuse, and she was shocked at what she learned.

"I can remember asking Emma what happened, and she told me he would try to choke her," Gail McCann said. "She [said] she had to leave. It was the only way."

Gail McCann said John Addis, the man she had known, had only shown her one side of him: a state trooper who gave the appearance, at least, of being a very loving father and a good husband. Behind the scenes, she later learned, he was abusive, controlling, and scary. She would later come to learn the abuse truly was severe. Gail is the type of person who would have done something immediately if she had known about the abuse, but she now knows, looking back, that she was not allowed to see the full John. She only got to see the side of him he wanted her to see.

"When the bottom fell out, [Emma later] opened up to us, and I was surprised and so sorry to find out it was happening to her," Gail McCann said. "Back then we didn't know [as much] about spousal abuse, and she didn't [tell me]."

Paul Bartlett noticed some little things at first, too, about the relationship between Addis and Emma. The woman he called "mother" seemed very submissive to John and said very little. She hardly spoke.

"He did not have electricity at that cabin, [but I do remember] John would have his wife get up, early in the morning, go out from that cabin [in the freezing cold and dark], and start his patrol car so it would be warm, and she just would do it," Bartlett said.

Fellow state trooper Roger McCoy can recall the first instance that caused him some concern. He watched one time as Emma washed the family's clothes "the old-fashioned way," in a washtub. He was struck by how hard she was working just to do the laundry. The woman was scrubbing the clothes by hand in a way that was reminiscent of the gold rush era—not the 1970s. McCoy didn't like what he was seeing, so he told Addis he was going to help him out. He had a used washer and dryer that worked perfectly fine. He would sell him the appliances dirt cheap. Fifty bucks, McCoy said, and he figured the move was a gesture Addis would appreciate.

He did not.

"I kept trying to tell him, 'Look, John, I have a washer and dryer in excellent shape. I just bought two new ones. I'll tell you what. I'll sell them to you both for fifty bucks,' and John said, 'No, we don't need one,'" McCoy recalled. "I was like, 'Oh come on, you've got water, a pump, [you can have] electricity,' and he still said no. Then, finally he decided he would do it."

McCoy delivered the appliances to the Addis home a short time later, and Emma was there to greet him with great appreciation and thanks. She was so thankful at the prospect of not having to wash clothes by hand.

"His wife thanked me for it right in front of him," McCoy said. "So while I'm out there, at the house to deliver them, he starts ranting and raving on her because she wanted this automatic washer and dryer. She wanted them, and he didn't. I talked to him about it, and he remained mad at both of us. It was stupid."

McCoy found the incident a little alarming, and he later concluded that Addis "was definitely abusive to his wife. I know he was verbally abusive. That's part of the abuse he put his family through, and it wasn't just his wife. It was his kids, too."

Bartlett, too, gained more access to the Addis home over time. The men got to know each other. Addis bought a new plane around this time, in approximately 1980, and he started working as a hunting guide and coordinating outdoor adventures using his new Cessna 185D. Jim McCann said he noticed Addis was becoming "very bold" in the way he flew his plane. He was a bush pilot who appeared to have no qualms whatsoever about landing his plane in the tightest of spots. Bartlett made the same observation—that John was getting very daring in the cockpit as he flew into the bush. He was taking bigger and bigger risks in the air.

Around the same time, Bartlett noticed something else. He, too, did not like at all how Addis was treating his wife. He described John's treatment of Emma as "overpowering and controlling."

"It didn't seem too unusual at first until a person really spent more time around him," Bartlett said. "You wouldn't detect it from him, that this was going on with his wife, unless you were right close around the family. He didn't allow a lot of outside access into the inner family.

"I had come to see a trait in John that I didn't care for, which was he was overpowering to his wife," Bartlett said. "He wouldn't go to town unless he knew where she was [before he left]. A very unnatural type of controlling environment. She would not say much to it. Just submit."

"Another thing I realized was that [Emma] was a registered nurse, a professional woman, yet he didn't want her working around other people at all."

It seemed to Bartlett the situation was getting a little strange. The interactions between the husband and wife, at first, were not overt as far as abuse was concerned, but Bartlett could feel in his stomach that something was not quite right between the husband and wife as time went on. The situation left him unsettled. Bartlett eventually decided he was going to say something to Addis about it even if it cost him his friendship. He was planning to confront his friend about the way he treated Emma, but before he did, Emma took the matter into her own hands.

In 1982, Emma picked up and left John Addis. She took the children and removed herself from the home. Addis's response was to immediately file for divorce, and Emma's friends said she kept a low profile out of pure fear. She would say later she left Addis because she had no choice. He was a perpetrator of terrifying acts of domestic violence when no one else was around.

It was either leave Addis or, she feared, he would kill her.

"He was [abusive]," Emma would later tell a Las Vegas grand jury. "A lot of shoving, hair pulling, pinning up against the wall with his hand to my throat. Grabbing my throat. I was never unconscious, but definitely it was enough to squeeze my neck. I would say [it started] shortly after we moved to Alaska."

Emma said Addis scared her. He was unstable at times and flew into rages against her over the smallest issue. When he was like this, he gave the appearance of being deranged, she said. She described him as extremely frightening.

"Physical abuse," Emma said of her marriage with Addis. "[It] included slapping, mostly shoving, pinning down to the ground or floor."

Addis "always said he was sorry" after the beatings, Emma said, yet the physical assaults got progressively worse.

"I was not allowed to have friends who might influence me," Emma told the *News-Miner* newspaper in Fairbanks. "He told me to sever ties with my family because they didn't care about me. I wasn't allowed to drive because I might have an accident.

"We didn't know what would set him off," she said.

Emma revealed to Bartlett as part of the divorce proceedings that when Addis got scary it was a very serious matter. These weren't just spousal arguments that got out of control out at the cabin. Emma revealed to Bartlett that Addis had beaten Emma and was threatening to kill himself. Bartlett was startled. He knew Addis was controlling. He did not know he'd been violent.

"The allegation was that John had threatened her with suicide if she didn't do what he said—that he would shoot himself in front of her and the kids," Bartlett said.

Bartlett was torn by the information he was receiving from Emma. There were times when he didn't know what to believe. He knew Addis. Addis was his friend, but as part of the divorce proceedings, Bartlett agreed to give a statement to Emma's attorneys, telling them that John was controlling. He'd never been a witness to any physical violence or threats of suicide, and he remained confused about what he should do. He hoped that Addis would come out of the divorce okay, that they could remain friends, and that Addis could still have a meaningful relationship with his children.

John Addis, meanwhile, was enraged that his wife had left him, and Bartlett said the divorce proceedings in Fairbanks "angered him bad." Then, Addis became even more angry when he learned that Emma's lawyer had secured a statement from Bartlett about how Addis treated his wife.

Bartlett agreed to give the statement to Emma's lawyer, on behalf of Emma, because he didn't like how Addis behaved toward the soft-spoken woman. Bartlett is an honest and upright man with a lengthy and successful career in law enforcement. He knew he had to tell the truth about how his friend treated Emma even if it resulted in the loss of his friendship with Addis. Addis, as Bartlett suspected, viewed the decision to give a statement to Emma's lawyers as the ultimate act of betrayal.

"They were separating, getting a divorce, and the tide actually turned with John when I sided with Emma during their divorce," Bartlett said. "I did that because I was able to see inside the marriage. A lot of guys didn't know how John really was, but I sided with her.

"It was a custody thing that angered John bad because he did love his children a lot, and he was good with children," Bartlett said. "But I was willing to give the statement because I had to do what is right. That's the way I felt about it. I wasn't going to protect him just because he was my best friend for a time."

Emma would later reveal more troubling and disturbing behavior exhibited by Addis. She would allege he tried to manipulate the children psychologically. Emma told authorities John would tell the children that they should tell everyone they wanted to live with him. At one point, he told his youngest son he might never see his sisters again because he was going to divide the siblings up as part of the divorce proceedings. Addis threatened Emma during the divorce, warning her not to fight for custody. He threatened to punish her severely if she did.

What he said next terrified her and struck fear in her heart.

"He, over the telephone, told me that if I did contest it, that he would take the children and put them in his private airplane and fly to the Brooks Range and crash them into the side of a mountain," Emma said.

Emma was terrified of Addis, and she did not want to let him have custody of the children. She returned to Fairbanks and fought in court like a tiger, but Addis was seeking custody. A settlement ensued, and she reluctantly agreed to the following terms: "Both parties agree that both husband and wife are fit and proper persons to have the custody, care and control of the minor children. The wife should be awarded the actual custody, care and control of the minor children, subject to the rights and responsibilities of visitation of husband."

The divorce was finalized in 1982. Addis received "liberal" visitation rights through the school year, according to Alaska court records, as long as he coordinated that visitation with Emma. He also received the children for up to six weeks a year in the summer.

Emma, although fearful of Addis, was stuck in a very difficult position as a result of the divorce order. The divorce was acrimonious, yet the children loved their father. She feared Addis, yet she had a court order indicating she regularly had to hand her children over to him for visitation and for six weeks in the summer. The court's ruling meant that Addis, for six weeks out of the year, would have complete control of her four children and would also be allowed to visit them on a regular basis.

"The children stayed at our residence, and, every two weeks, went back and forth," Emma would tell a grand jury in Fairbanks of the school-year visitation and exchanges by

Addis of the children from Emma's home to Addis's home on weekends.

"That way, the children would be in their home," Emma said.

Emma knew Addis was filled with hate for her.

She knew he had a dark side.

And she was afraid that, one day, he might do something crazy.

7 ... EVERYTHING SLIPS AWAY/

GOING SIDEWAYS

John Addis, in a period of a couple of years, witnessed his entire personal life unravel. The woman he'd come to Alaska with, the mother of his children, had left him and told everyone he was an unstable psycho who scared her. Despite this, there is no indication in the public record that Addis's job was ever threatened by supervisors at the Alaska Department of Public Safety. Jim McCann, meanwhile, did not learn of Emma's allegations of abuse by John until years after the fact. McCann said Addis was clearly bitter about the divorce. He was not the type of man who was used to being challenged in his personal life, and losing his children for most of the year clearly impacted him in a negative way.

"I think the scuttlebutt was he wanted to blame another trooper for the divorce and claim that that was why—that there was another trooper with his wife," McCann said. "In retrospect, I think she got strong and left him."

Addis denied the allegations attributed to him during the divorce and nasty custody dispute, but friends of Addis say the turn of events for the trooper was clearly devastating. He was more abrupt at work. He was frosty with both McCann and Bartlett. Addis, it seemed, was starting to withdraw. He didn't want to talk about forensics anymore. He didn't want to chat over a cup of coffee about which trooper had arrested which suspect the night before. He seemed generally disinterested in the type of stuff cops talked about, and he didn't talk about hunting and fishing as much anymore. People started watching Addis a little more closely at the state trooper barracks, and Bartlett said they "were all starting to notice" the change in Addis's behavior.

"He got divorced," Jim McCann said. "We started growing apart, and I was moving on. I was loaded up with [homicide] cases, and he had some other people in his life he was flying around with.

"I didn't ask him [about the divorce], and he wasn't one to sit around and talk," McCann said. "For some reason, he didn't like me anymore, but he had to deal with me because he worked for me."

Bartlett suspects Addis was losing it. John liked to have control over everything involving Emma. Now, she was out of his life and in possession of his children. He no longer had any say over what she did. He was only allowed to see his four children during summer visitation and every two weeks, when he coordinated with Emma. Their communications were tense, and she would later accuse him of attempting to manipulate the children psychologically. He was not allowed to be around Emma at all, and friends said it enraged him deeply. One thing about John, Bartlett said, was that he was a man who wanted to control everything. To not have that control over his family life was, in retrospect, something his friends say eventually caused him to go "completely nuts" in a violent and dangerous way.

"I bet he was angry," McCann said. "Things were really unraveling for him."

Still, for a little more than a year, there were mostly signs Addis was going to try to hold on and to rebuild his life. He continued to work as a trooper even though he'd become more reserved and less chummy with his friends. During that first year, with custody of the kids, there were no major incidents as John and Emma shuttled the kids to and from each other's homes in Fairbanks so that Addis could get his parenting time in.

In 1982, Addis made a surprising announcement to his friends: he'd met a new woman—Sarah Rayder.* She was a very attractive blond who worked as a secretary at the Fairbanks Office of Fish and Wildlife. Addis told his friends they were in love. Rayder was a woman with children from a prior marriage, and Addis had his children for visitation for a period of weeks every year. The two could relate to each other as single parents. Addis purportedly doted over Rayder's kids and treated her with great respect early in the relationship. He was trying to build a new family, this time with Rayder's kids and his four children every few weeks coming in and going out of the home. Friends were surprised to learn that, despite having only recently met, Addis and Rayder were planning to marry.

Bartlett knew Rayder. When he heard she was going to marry Addis, he was convinced she was not aware of the domestic-abuse allegations made against Addis by his first wife. He felt he should tell her in case she hadn't heard about the accusations. If she already knew about the allegations that Addis had slapped and choked his wife, fine; but she needed to know before she got further involved with Addis.

"I said, 'Sarah, I don't know whether you have any idea about your involvement with John,'" Bartlett recalled. "I said, 'I know you are a woman who thinks he is in love with you,' but I told her . . . that I'd feared for Emma, and I told her John had threatened [Emma] with suicide if she didn't do what he said. That he would shoot himself in front of her and the kids. I told her that, and she said, 'I can't believe it. He's so nice to my kids.'

"I said, 'Sarah, I'm sure he loves the children, but the problem isn't with the kids,'" Bartlett recalled. "I said, 'If there's [going to be a problem], it's [going to be] with you.'"

Rayder and Addis married despite the warning, and the two moved into a nice suburban home in Fairbanks.

"I was administrative assistant [for Alaska state government] in 1980, and we married in December of 1982," Rayder would later say.

The couple, Rayder said, married in the home of a former magistrate in Alaska whom she described as a friend of Addis's. She did not identify him by name.

Jim McCann was surprised by the marriage and the ongoing transformation of John from a man who'd lived in a cabin with no running water, no electricity, and an outhouse to a man who was living in suburbia and starting to act more and more like the other troopers in a more traditional, domestic, suburban lifestyle that included daily trips to the grocery store, jaunts in the park, and walking one's dog. It just didn't seem like John, but there he was, trying to fit in.

"Now he's married to this woman, and she is very prim and proper, and they are living in a house with a picket fence on River View Drive in Fairbanks," McCann said.

The new developments and surprises in Addis's life didn't stop there, however; Addis soon told his friends that after nearly eight years as a state trooper and after being trained in and learning all the most modern techniques for crime-scene investigation and processing, he was going to quit the state police. He was resigning his job as investigator. He wanted to do something different, he said, and he was going to go back to medical school.

"Then, all of a sudden, something happened," McCann said. "He started spreading the rumor and told the command he was leaving the troopers and going back to medical school. He was gonna go back to medical school, and a lot of people were shaking his hand and saying good-bye. All of a sudden, he's leaving the force."

Roger McCoy was shocked to learn Addis was quitting the state troopers. He saw Addis as an extremely talented investigator. Addis had spent years honing his skills as a forensics expert. He'd trained for years on the SWAT team. He was a man who could fly a plane into the bush, and that was a valuable asset to have as a state cop. Now, McCoy learned, Addis was turning his back on the force and moving on.

"He went sideways, and he quit," McCoy said. "I was surprised because he was a good investigator, no doubt about it. He solved a lot of crimes."

His colleagues were stunned, but they also knew that Addis had struggled badly after his divorce. He at times was distant and unhappy. With this new development, some of his fellow troopers decided to throw him a going-away party at a buddy's house. Bartlett recalls attending a little going-away event put on by a friend, Steve Heckman.

McCann specifically recalls Addis showing his colleagues "a letter [of acceptance] from the dean of some medical school" in Florida.

Addis seemed very intent on showing his letter of acceptance to medical school to everyone he could. He said he and his new bride were moving to Florida, where he was going to study to become a doctor.

"We had the party for John, and he told everyone, again, he was going to go away to medical school," Bartlett said.

The next thing everyone knew, within five months, after the move to Florida with her new husband, Sarah returned to Fairbanks without Addis.

She'd divorced him.

"She divorced him very quickly, and then we started to hear some things, rumors about him going off the deep end," Gail McCann said. "[We heard] he was acting crazy."

"I'm thankful that she figured it out before something serious happened," Bartlett said. "I think he did exactly what he did to Emma. Pulled a gun on her or himself and threatening to kill. He was just getting progressively worse."

McCoy, too, suspected his friend had started to become unstable.

Then word started to circulate throughout Fairbanks that Addis never went to medical school. There was a rumor flying around that the letter from the dean was a complete fabrication.

"I subsequently found out it was all just a big lie,"

Bartlett said. "Not that he wasn't extremely capable of [going to medical school], but I later learned it was all just a big ruse."

McCann also heard about the medical-school ruse and learned that the letter of acceptance from the dean had been forged. This was the moment that Addis's fellow state troopers concluded that he was officially losing it. His behavior was bizarre, bordering on crazy. There was no reason for the deceit about medical school and the forgery of the letter. If Addis wanted to quit being a state trooper, he could have just done so. The idea of going to such trouble to fake a reason for his departure from the Alaska Department of Public Safety seemed truly bizarre, and no one was able to account for it. Both McCann and Bartlett were alarmed. It seemed to them that Addis was having a hard time crafting a new life after a bitter divorce. The fake college letter and the failure to go to medical school were signs of his instability. The John Addis who was lying to his colleagues as part of an escape from his old life in Alaska was a far cry from the man they'd known when they'd all started working together.

The respected crime-scene investigator was now acting completely crazy, and his friends were concerned that he had gone over the edge.

"[At first we] thought he just went off the deep end because of the divorce, but looking back, I don't think anyone really understood how deeply distressed he was," Bartlett said.

Roger McCoy decided his former friend was losing it, and Jim McCann was amazed at Addis's downfall. He no longer seemed to be the same person McCoy had come to know.

"There was a time where I really loved that guy, and then, all of a sudden, he's off in another world," McCann said.

Sarah Rayder would also reveal something else about Addis. During their brief marriage, she noticed some very unstable behavior. She said Addis would "disappear for weeks," and no one would know where he was. He refused to explain where he'd been when he returned. Addis, she said, was "obsessed" with having his children. She told of an incident in January 1983 in Fairbanks in which Addis took his kids from their home and kept them for days.

"He went to their home while we were still living in Fairbanks and said that he had to have his children," she recalled. "He brought them to the home—took them while a babysitter was in the home and the mother was at work. Brought them to our home and then they remained there for two days."

The incident caused extensive friction between Emma and John. Sarah said the holding of the children was bothersome enough, but she knew something was truly wrong with John when he confided to her that he was planning on committing a serious crime. He wanted to steal all four of his children from his marriage with Emma, and he asked Rayder if she would help. She was absolutely stunned at the request.

"He was planning to kidnap them [because] he needed to have them with him," Rayder would tell law enforcement years later.

Rayder said Addis was apparently plotting to pose as a woman and steal the children while they were with a babysitter. Disguising himself as a woman would possibly prevent witnesses from recognizing him while he was kidnapping the children and, afterward, while he was fleeing.

"He stored clothing . . . and he would be posing as a woman," she said. "He would dress as a woman, shave his legs, and take on the appearance of a woman.

"He would . . . dress up like a woman, and go into the home, and tie up the babysitter if necessary and take the children," she said. "He would take the children, possibly to Australia or Canada. He was going to take them from their mother. I found out after the fact he'd requested copies of blank birth certificates from a gal that worked in [state government]. He owned an airplane. I assumed he would put them on the plane and they would go. He asked me if I would help him do it, and I said, 'Absolutely not!' And I told him he was crazy, that it would never happen. He told me it was his plan and then asked if I would join him, that he had to at least have me tell him that I would join him in Australia or Canada, to which I replied, 'No, that wouldn't happen.' "

"He said he would have to resort to that . . . and that was his plan," Rayder recalled. "He disappeared once for three weeks and that was the time I thought he was planning to take them. And, when he returned, nobody knew where he was for that three-week period. Nobody had heard from him. But, he was planning to go and find a place to keep them."

Rayder went to file for divorce from Addis a short time after the conversation about the kidnapping plot.

"I went for a divorce [and found] the marriage license was never filed, so, legally, we were never married as far as the courts were concerned," Rayder said.

John and Emma had divorced in 1982. That same year,

Addis had married Rayder only to see that marriage fall apart after moving to Florida. By 1983, when he was exchanging custody of the children with Emma, Addis was becoming very difficult to deal with. In the next eighteen months, he would get married yet again, to Toni Martinez,* and all the while, Addis bickered with his first wife over the exchange of the children and, after the move to Florida, where they would spend their visitation time—in Fairbanks or Florida. On one visitation in which Addis picked up the children and took them on a bus trip, Emma reportedly went to court and had Addis post a bond "just to assure me that they would come back." What Emma described as a very difficult and long bus ride for the children to Michigan followed, but Addis returned the children without incident.

8 ... FLORIDA

Toni Martinez is a professional, attractive woman who has lived most of her life in Florida. In April 1984, she was working as a pharmacist in the Sarasota area when a friend told her he'd met a man at a gym that she might like. He was big, strong, very handsome, respectful, outgoing, and kind. The friend told her he wanted to set Martinez up with the man, and his name was John Patrick Addis.

Martinez immediately found Addis to be a very handsome man. He was just as her friend had described: he was strong, physically fit, and didn't do drugs. He was working as a mortgage broker in Sarasota. She knew he'd been married twice before, but over time, the two started to date. Addis told her he'd been in law enforcement in Alaska, that he'd been through a terrible divorce with his first ex-wife, and that he'd come to Florida for a fresh start. He said he had four children from his first marriage, and he only had custody of them for six weeks every year.

Martinez decided to give him a chance.

"Late spring, early summer, 1984, we started dating," Martinez would later tell a Las Vegas grand jury. "You know, we became close to each other, intimate with each other."

She found Addis to be especially intriguing because he was a survivalist, hunter, and pilot who flew her all over the continental United States in his airplane. He seemed just like Bear Grylls in the *Man vs. Wild* television show. He could survive in extreme conditions. He told stories of being dropped off in the mountains of Alaska and surviving for days with few supplies. He was very different from any man she'd ever known. He wasn't interested in going to the bars or clubs. He was into physical fitness, and he wanted to be outdoors. He had a small Cessna, and sometimes he would rent a historic 1942 airplane and fly her off on romantic, days-long vacations.

"We flew together actually [to] several places," Martinez said. "We went around quite a bit. He had many years' experience flying single-engine aircraft, and he was actually quite good at it. He was very good in a pinch. A very daring kind of person.

"We flew all around Florida," Martinez said. "We [flew] to Key West. The Bahamas. We flew from Alaska to Michigan in a very small, 1942 aircraft, I believe it was. Just he and I. He piloted the plane through storms, and we had breakdowns. We repaired the plane ourselves, you know."

Martinez would later say she had a very strange conversation with Addis about his children from his first marriage. The two were talking about children and family, and Addis made a shocking revelation to her. He told Martinez he'd previously vetted a plot to steal his kids.

"He had told me he had made a plan for kidnapping his children," Martinez recalled. "He owned a couple airplanes, he had altered the registration number on one of the airplanes, and changed the number. He had tried to acquire blank birth certificates for the four children, and he had practiced flying 'low and slow,' as he called it, over the Canadian border to avoid detection.

"He disappeared for a period of time before he was to attempt it," Martinez said. "Then, he told me of how he had flown through Canadian airspace . . . to see if he could do it before he actually was going to make the attempt. He had mentioned something about going to Australia. I don't know if he ever actually purchased tickets, or if he had intended to do so at some point, but he had mentioned Australia."

Martinez was stunned by the conversation. Addis talked about the plot in the past tense, as if it was something he'd decided against. He and Martinez later traveled to Alaska for the purpose of visiting his children. Martinez found the children to be sweet, beautiful, and very smart. She could see why Addis talked about them and had even contemplated taking them. They were beautiful children, and she knew he was angry he didn't have primary custody of the kids. In fact, he was very bitter about it.

Emma, meanwhile, found the process of turning her children over to Addis for six weeks a year to be a truly miserable and frightening experience. Addis had, in fits of anger, threatened to cause harm to himself and the children. After years of experiencing John's violent temper and physical abuse, Emma knew all too well the violence and manipulation John was capable of. He could be downright terrifying. She knew how he could morph into a very

frightening individual when he was upset, yet despite her
pleas to the court, Addis was basically allowed to decide
where he took the children during his visitation time. He
rarely informed Emma of his plans. It was a very frustrating situation that the Alaska family courts had essentially
endorsed. Each year, Emma spent those six weeks worrying and wondering about the safety of her children.

"He wasn't real good at communicating," Emma said.
"He would communicate with me through my oldest
daughter. And, when I would tell him, 'I'd rather talk to
you directly,' he didn't want that to happen. [He would not
get on the phone] unless I insisted, and then he [wouldn't
talk]. Very briefly, 'Well, this is what I'm going to do.' "

Addis proposed to Martinez, and she accepted. They
married after less than a year of dating. The couple's
daughter, Sheila,* was born in September 1985.

Martinez had assumed Addis had given up on the idea
of kidnapping his kids. She'd strongly told Addis that he
should do no such thing—that it was a terrible idea and that
although she understood that he loved the children, stealing them was not the answer. If he dared to follow through
with the plan, she would have no part of it. She also warned
him that if he got caught, he would end up in prison. Addis
had previously told her he'd dropped the idea, playing it off
as a half-assed joke born out of frustration from his miserable divorce.

The children later visited the couple in Florida in 1985
for six weeks, and Martinez watched Addis engage in some
rather manipulative behavior with the children. In one
instance, Addis caused his young son, Richard Franklin, to
break out in tears of grief and sorrow. She questioned the

child as to why he was so upset and learned that Addis had told the child he was never going to "see his sisters again."

Martinez told an Alaskan grand jury that Richard Franklin feared his sisters "were probably going to live with their father, but that he had to go home with his mother . . . so he would never see them again."

Addis was continually telling the children to tell their mother that they didn't want to come back to Alaska. They should tell Emma, he said, that they wanted to live in Florida with him. The children ended up telling Emma this in what was a very painful episode for their mother. Emma knew, however, that they didn't really mean it—that John had put them up to it.

"About two weeks before they were supposed to come home, we had preplanned that they would call me designated days," Emma said. "And, then, two weeks before they were supposed to come home, they started in with, 'We want to stay here! . . . We want to stay in Florida with Dad, it's really nice down here, he has a pool, the weather's nice and warm.' And I told them, each one individually, that they were there for a vacation, and they were there to visit their dad. I was glad they were having a good time, but that they would be coming home in two weeks."

Emma was incensed and immediately demanded that Addis get on the phone.

"I told him if he didn't stop trying to influence them, I would come and get them at that time, and he would only have a four-week visit," she said.

Martinez noticed a change in Addis around this time. During the 1985 visit from the children, she started to become concerned that maybe Addis hadn't let go of the idea of taking the kids, and Addis became more controlling toward Martinez. He wanted to know where she was at all times. When she went to work, he would follow her. He checked her odometer to see how far she'd driven during the workday. Then, over time, John became physically violent, and it scared her. The violence usually surfaced in the middle of a heated argument, and Addis would start to wrestle, smother, or choke her around the neck.

"He would grab me, kind of pin me down, and not let me move," Martinez said. "One time he grabbed me by the throat and pushed me up against the wall and lifted me off my feet and was choking me. I was having difficulty breathing."

She was terrified by his behavior, yet she stayed with him. She loved him, and she also feared him. In yet another domestic dispute, Martinez and Addis "actually got into a physical fight where we actually fought with each other. Actually wrestled. I was hitting and kicking him, and he was trying to pin me down and throwing me around."

She soon concluded she would divorce Addis. He had, at first, seemed like the perfect man. It was only after they married that she saw him for what he was—a truly frightening individual who wanted complete control over her. The episode that led to her filing for divorce came in October 1985. Martinez was at the home she shared with Addis, feeding their newborn baby, when Addis stormed into the room unprovoked, "ranting and raving."

Martinez was terrified by the expression she saw on Addis's face. He looked raving mad. Deranged, even.

"He approached me, stepped on my feet with his feet, grabbed me by the hair and pulled me up out of the chair and shook me around," Martinez said. "The bottle went flying out of my hands. Sheila started crying. He was going on and on. Finally, he released me. He pushed me back, and then he left the house."

Martinez immediately left the home and filed for an order for protection, which she received. Before she could file for divorce, Addis did. Addis was never arrested for domestic violence, however, and he was, during the initial stages of the divorce proceedings, able to secure visitation with Sheila while the divorce was pending.

The next month, while Martinez was staying with an aunt, she received a call from John. He wanted to see the baby. Martinez reluctantly agreed to the request.

"John had called me and asked me if he could go to my house and see her," Martinez recalled. "It was not a scheduled visit. I called my aunt and asked her if it was okay if he came when I wasn't there, and she said yes."

An hour passed, and Martinez received a frantic call from her aunt. Addis had left the home with the baby. Martinez, paralyzed with fear, immediately called the police. She met detectives, and they drove to Addis's Sarasota home. He was found inside the home with Sheila. The baby was unharmed.

Amazingly, Addis was not arrested, and he described the incident to police as a big misunderstanding.

"I went with [the police] to John's house, where he was with my daughter," Martinez said. "They went in the residence and brought her out."

Like Emma in Alaska, she continued to be stuck with having to deal with Addis and allowing him visitation with her daughter.

In the divorce proceedings, only two assets were at issue: a home and truck. The home, on Beneva Road in

Sarasota, was purchased by Addis, and he continued to live in the home throughout the summer but stopped making payments in June of that year. Martinez, meanwhile, had fled the home with their daughter and was living with family.

A gray pickup truck was in Martinez's name. Martinez was continuing to make payments on the vehicle, but it remained in Addis's possession. Martinez was frustrated at her inability to get the truck back from Addis even though the truck was in her name. She told him she wanted the truck back, "but that didn't do me any good," she said, and Addis acted throughout the summer as if the truck was his, and yet he still expected her to continue making the payments. Martinez, fearing Addis, tried to do as little as possible to cause confrontation with Addis during the divorce.

In August 1986, Martinez noticed during Addis's visitation with her daughter that Addis was building a camper for the back of her pickup. She asked him what he was doing. He explained that the camper was for the next time the children visited Florida. Addis told her they would probably be going camping for a while.

In August 1986, Addis made a brief comment to her that his children from Alaska were coming for a "special" visitation that month.

That same month, Addis and the pickup disappeared.

Martinez would never see John Patrick Addis again.

In August 1986, it was time for John Addis to receive his annual six weeks with his four children from Alaska. He was still living in Florida at that time. His ex-wife Emma was now remarried to a man in Fairbanks who treated her with respect and dignity. Addis, meanwhile, was the man who had terrorized her. Emma wanted him to come to Alaska to visit the children, but Addis refused, saying it "would cost too much money." Emma was also alarmed because Addis wanted the children in August. There was no way he could have them for an entire six weeks without them missing school. She went to court to make sure Addis was going to have the children back for the beginning of the school year, and she wanted him to be fully responsible for getting the children from Alaska to Sarasota. Addis would also be responsible for getting the children on an airplane back to Alaska when the visitation was up. Addis notified the court he was ready for the children, and Emma prepared for the psychological torment that came with having to give her four children over to a man who'd tormented her. Her children were easily the most important thing to her in her life. She loved them very, very dearly, and she was very close to them.

She feared it was at least possible that Addis might use the children as a weapon against her. He'd already shown he was willing to try and hurt Emma through the children. In one instance in 1986, Emma's oldest daughter, Charlotte, got a call from her father. Emma noticed the child crying while she was on the phone. Tears were streaming down the girl's face. Emma was heartbroken at the sight. Emma sneaked off to another area of her home, picked up another receiver, and listened in on a very brief snippet of conversation between father and daughter.

"She was on the telephone in the kitchen, and we have an extension in the master bedroom," Emma said. "I picked up the phone and heard him say to her, 'If you don't do this, you'll never see me again!' And, at that point, I said, 'John, you don't have any right to tell her that.' Because, obviously, whatever he was saying to her was upsetting to her."

Addis was being totally uncooperative with her that summer—she'd wanted to try to work something out to change the dates of the visitation so the children could attend another family function in Fairbanks, but Addis would have none of it. Addis, who had worked a number of different jobs—selling water softeners, working as a private detective, and being a mortgage broker—wanted the children in August, and he wanted them to come to Florida. He wanted to have the children in the last three weeks of the summer, in the days leading right up to the time the children were to return to school in September. Emma thought it was not appropriate to put that much stress on the children.

"The divorce granted me custody of the children with him getting six weeks visitation, and it was time for visitation," Emma said. "At the time, he was living in Florida, and I had approached the court to say, you know, 'I'm very uncomfortable with this,' but they reminded me that's the way the decree read, and that's what I had to do."

Emma said a hearing was scheduled for August 8, 1986, on whether Addis's parental visitation time should be reduced. Emma told newspapers she received a court notice on August 7, 1986, giving her just a day's notice for the hearing that would delve into Addis's rushed plan for a three-week-long visitation to Florida by the children for the remaining weeks of August. According to the *Fairbanks Daily News-Miner*, she attended the hearing alone because she couldn't get in touch with her attorney. An attorney for Addis said Addis should not be forced to come to Alaska to visit the kids that summer. Instead, they should be flown to the continental United States.

"I told the judge, if [John] took the children out of state, I didn't think they'd come back," Emma told the newspaper of the warning she had issued during the hearing.

Nonetheless, the judge ordered Addis to buy round-trip tickets, and he ordered Emma to put the children on a plane to Florida once round-trip tickets had been purchased. Emma tried to protest, but the judge would have none of it.

"I don't deny the fact that the children need contact with their father, but he's at times real unreasonable, real hard to come to agreements or workable agreements with," Emma told the judge during the August 8 hearing. "This new thing about wanting them the last three weeks [before] school, you know, unless he wants to come [to Fairbanks], I don't see how I can pull them up and get them back and ready for school to start when it does start the end of August, the first part of September. I'm not trying to be unreasonable. It was me who tried to initiate some kind of arrangements this year. And he just didn't want to do that."

"Very well, anything further?" the judge said in the hearing before ordering the visitation to Florida and the purchase of the round-trip tickets.

"Your honor, since we're on the subject, another thing about the child support payments," Emma said.

"We're not on that subject," the judge said.

"But this man can have visitation with his children and he doesn't pay any of the bills," Emma said.

"You can file a motion," the judge said.

"The children ought to have summer vacation in Florida," the judge said. "Departure as soon as the tickets are here for them to go. They do need to be returned in time to start school in the fall; [there] should be no efforts on the part of Mr. Addis to convince the children to remain in Florida during the visitation. And the tickets should be round-trip, of course, when they get there."

The judge then instructed Mr. Addis's attorney: "Tell Mr. Addis exactly what I've said. If there are any efforts to interfere with the children being in Fairbanks, it's just going [to make this] more difficult every year."

After the hearing, Emma was contacted by Addis's attorney, John Ensminger, and she learned Addis had purchased only one-way tickets to Florida for the kids. Her daughter told her, " 'You know, dad says he's going to drive us back to Alaska this year,' " Emma recounted for the Alaska grand jury. "And I said, 'Oh wait a minute. That's not what the court said.' "

She later confronted Addis over the phone about the one-way tickets.

"I spoke with him and said, 'You know, the judge has ordered me to allow the children to come, to go [to the] Outside,' " Emma recalled of her conversation with Addis, using the term *Outside* for trips to the continental United States. "And he's ordered you to provide round-trip airfare. So, you know, I have to follow what the judge says, so do you. He said, 'Well, I don't have the money,' and I said, 'Well, I'm sorry but that's what the judge ordered.' "

Emma demanded proof from her ex-husband that there were round-trip tickets for the children, and he later confirmed to her that he'd purchased return tickets for the children.

"They were supposed to leave on United Airlines, and I called the airlines to make sure that there was a round-trip airfare," Emma said. "And I was told that there was."

Court documents indicate Addis had approached a Florida travel agent to purchase the tickets for the kids' return trip to Alaska. He got the tickets, but the check Addis wrote for the return tickets bounced, and the travel agent testified Addis "never made an attempt" to pick up the return tickets at the United Airlines counter. None of this was known to Emma when she put her four children on the one-way flight Addis had booked for them to Chicago.

It is not clear why they flew to Chicago. Addis had family in Michigan, however, and likely was planning to take the children there.

"I had prearranged with Charlotte, who is the oldest, that we would talk every Wednesday," Emma would later tell Las Vegas authorities. "I think it was once a week, at least, mainly because I wanted to be reassured that they were where they should be. . . . They called when they first got to Chicago."

Emma worried intensely, but at first, at least, everything went off as planned. It wasn't until late in the visitation, during a phone call from the children on August 27, that Emma learned there was no return flight after all.

"It was my little one's birthday, and I [had been] told they were going to spend it in Michigan with their grand-parents," Emma said. "And . . . I talked to all of them, and asked where they were, and their responses were, 'I don't know.' And I said, 'What do you mean you don't know?' And [Charlotte] said, 'Well, we're in a motel. [Susan Leigh] wanted to spend her birthday in a motel.' And I said, 'Okay, that's fine: where is the motel?' And it was, 'I don't know. In Canada someplace.' So, I asked to speak with my ex-husband and he refused to talk with me. So, I continued to talk to the rest of the children . . . and again, I asked, 'Let me talk to your dad.' He refused. [Then] I finally did find out from them they were in a motel in Ontario. [Charlotte] said that their father didn't have a return ticket. And, I said, '[Charlotte], there is a return ticket. I called United Airlines before you left. And there is one, and it's waiting for you in Chicago, and even if you are in Ontario, you have plenty of time to get back here before September first.' It was the day they were supposed to fly back. And, she said, 'Well, dad said there isn't one, and so he's going to bring us home.' And I said, 'Okay, if he's changing his plans, then I want you children to call me every day at noon, no matter where you are' . . . so it would be easy for them to remember."

Charlotte was now thirteen. Mary Beth was eleven. Richard Franklin was six, and Susan Leigh was five. The youth of the children, along with their requirement to travel such great distances to be with Addis, caused Emma to fret throughout the week. She heard nothing from the children even though she'd asked them to call every day at noon. When the date for the children's return finally arrived, on September 1, Emma drove to the airport with her husband, and her worst fears were realized. She stood in the airport terminal in Fairbanks, watching passenger after passenger flying in from Chicago and exiting down the ramp and into the terminal.

"And, when it came time for them to be on their return flight, my husband and I met the plane, and they weren't on it," Emma said.

9 ... TORMENT

Emma frantically checked with United Airlines clerks and learned the children had never even boarded the return flight from Chicago. A very deep-seated dread of the worst kind flooded through Emma. John, she knew, had stolen the children. She was broken to the core by the tormenting crime. Her children were missing and in the hands of her ex-husband, and she felt completely powerless to do anything about it. She hoped it was just a misunderstanding, but deep inside, she knew immediately that John had stolen the children, and she was brokenhearted, terrified, and angry over the fate of her missing kids. John was exerting his control over her by kidnapping the children. He'd previously threatened to kill them during the custody dispute; now he was continuing to abuse her long after the days of the remote, difficult life they'd lived in Goldstream Valley, north of Fairbanks.

She and her husband called the police immediately.

"I called the local authorities, and they said that not enough time had elapsed, and I had to wait twenty-four hours before I could do that, and I did," Emma would later tell Las Vegas law enforcement.

She and her new husband hoped the children would show up the next day. Perhaps Addis was playing games and would send them home a day late, but they didn't show up, Emma said. Emma repeatedly went to local and state police in Alaska, telling them how although Addis had promised her and the court that he'd bought round-trip tickets, she found out later there were no return tickets. She said at first there was some reluctance to launch a major search for Addis because of his background in local law enforcement. This was also decades before the world of AMBER Alerts, massive police responses, bulletins on interstates, and cable television alerting the world anytime a child goes missing. On September 1, Emma attempted to report the children missing but faced a series of obstacles from the get-go. She was not in possession of a physical copy of the court order because it was Labor Day, the *Fairbanks Daily News-Miner* reported. She learned the next day the order was not filed. She bought a taped copy of the hearing from the court in which it was stated that Addis was supposed to have the children back in time for school, but the police "wouldn't even listen to it," she told the *News-Miner* in 1986. "They rolled their eyes and said, 'Oh no, another one.' I had to fight with the police to take my report."

"No one should have to go through this," Emma told the *News-Miner*.

Devastated and angry, Emma committed herself to conducting a national search for her children. A city detective eventually assisted her, and a friend got in touch with

Alaska senator Frank Murkowski's office. He, in turn, brought in the help of a U.S. marshal in Michigan. Emma suspected Addis had gone back to Michigan with the children—perhaps into the Upper Peninsula.

"I contacted relatives, family members, anyone who knew him, police departments in areas where I thought they might be," Emma said. "I took leave of my job for six weeks and went back to Michigan looking for them. It was definitely nationwide.

"I contacted Missing Children, got them involved," Emma told a Las Vegas grand jury. "I sent some things . . . to Canada."

Emma learned in Michigan that Addis was suspected of stealing sixteen thousand dollars in tools from his uncle in Houghton, Michigan, the place of the couple's marriage in 1971.

Addis and the children were later spotted by a witness in Calumet, just across the canal and up the road from Houghton, on September 15, 1986. Michigan state police put out a Michigan Law Enforcement Bulletin at the request of Fairbanks police. It read:

The Calumet Michigan state police post is assisting the Fairbanks, Alaska, Police Department in locating and attempting to apprehend John Patrick Addis. White male, six feet two inches tall, one hundred ninety five pounds, average build, sandy blond hair, short, full beard. The beard was observed when he was seen in Calumet, Michigan on 9-15-86. Addis is being sought on a felony warrant charging second-degree custodial interference [parental kidnapping] which is being held by Alaska authorities, who will extradite in lieu of fifty thousand dollars bond. Addis is also wanted on a warrant charging burglary and larceny over one hundred dollars, which is being held by the Houghton County, Michigan, Sheriff's Department, involving a sixteen thousand dollar equipment theft, which occurred on September fifteenth.

Addis is a former Alaska state trooper and private detective from the state of Florida. He is a private pilot and an accomplished woodsman. He has owned numerous firearms in the past and is very possibly armed. A former supervisor of the Alaska state police advised that he believes that Addis would shoot a police officer to prevent police from taking custody of his children. In early August of this year, Addis had a court-ordered thirty-day custody of his children. Addis failed to return the children to their mother in Fairbanks on September second. Addis and three of the children were identified in Calumet, Michigan, on September fifteenth. They were traced to Flint, Michigan, where they were identified and last seen at the Flint Greyhound Bus Terminal on September sixteenth.

Addis [has also been observed] driving a Ford F-250 pickup, two-tone, gray in color, with homemade camper, bearing Florida registration. Addis is connected with two aircraft that are now missing. One is a 1942 Aeronica [sic] four passenger tail dragger, orange and yellow, presently missing from a small airport near Brighton, Michigan. The second is a 185-Cessna, six passenger, white with red trim, which is now missing from Florida. Addis has many close relatives, including his parents and friends, living in Michigan.

The allegation of the stolen tools in Houghton was enough to get a federal warrant for unlawful flight to avoid prosecution. It was then that the FBI got involved. Emma suspected Addis had gone back to Michigan with the children—perhaps into the Upper Peninsula. The *Jackson Citizen Patriot* newspaper picked up the story of the woman whose children were stolen by the fugitive ex-cop.

"A former Jackson woman is home from Alaska on a desperate mission—to find her four children, who never returned from an August visit with her ex-husband," staff writer Patt Ciokajlo wrote.

Michigan state trooper Robert Swackhamer told the newspaper Addis was an outdoorsman who "could be very difficult to find."

"He's a survivalist," Swackhamer said. "He knows how to live in the bush. The children spent half their lives in the bush."

"I'm afraid for their safety," Emma told the paper.

The article reported Addis's parents saw their son and grandchildren on September 19. The father and children left Milford a day later with a "load of camping gear."

The *Fairbanks Daily News-Miner* newspaper picked up the story as well.

"Authorities now say Addis's two private planes are missing. The three youngest children were last seen on a bus in Flint, Michigan. It is believed the oldest child is traveling separately with [a companion of Addis's]."

"He has a problem and needs help," Emma told the paper. "He might have told the little ones that I was in an accident and was not there anymore," Emma said. "He would make up hundreds of different excuses."

"If I could just talk to them," she said, choking back tears in an interview with the newspaper. "My kids—they're my life."

"There was local publicity," Emma later told a Las Vegas grand jury. "The Fairbanks area picked it up. Michigan picked it up. I don't know where else it may have been, but I tried to get flyers out to as many places as I could think of."

John Addis was the type of person who could survive anywhere. He'd already built his own house in Alaska. He could hunt and fish to feed his family. He'd disappeared for weeks at a time during his second and third marriages. The speculation was that he had been out in the wilderness somewhere, prepping the kidnapping plot. He could fly a plane anywhere. He was increasingly fearless and unstable. He knew how police tracked people. He was a former cop himself.

Jim McCann described Addis's disappearance with his four children as downright mysterious. In addition to the sightings of Addis in Michigan, there were reported sightings of Addis in Alaska as well. McCann said he heard a report of a sighting of Addis with his plane in Alaska after the father and children vanished. There were rumors and speculation in late September and early October that perhaps Addis was in the bush somewhere.

"We turn on the television channel [and we hear about this] bizarre series of events [and] that there'd been no flight plan," Jim McCann said of an unconfirmed media report indicating Addis was somehow in Alaska with his plane. "There was a witness report of seeing him in Ketchikan, but there was no flight plan filed, and he flew off into the fog and rain and clouds. A witness saw him there fueling up. Other people [thought he'd left the state]. [He] might have crashed; then there was [a rumor that] he was supposed to be a suspect in burglaries in and around Michigan."

Perhaps he had crashed the plane somewhere. No one had any idea where they were, and Emma was left to wonder whether she would ever see her children alive again.

Taking the children and simply disappearing was clearly designed to torment Emma. Gail McCann, to this day, expresses extreme sorrow and sympathy for Emma over this terrible experience. Enduring such meanness and cruelty at the hands of her ex-husband is unimaginable.

"He went into hiding," Gail McCann said. "It was at a time when [spouses] were just starting to do that—taking kids—and it was on *Geraldo* [and those type of] stories."

Remarkably, Emma would be put through eight long months of torment not knowing where her children were. It was as if they'd vanished off the face of the earth. The crime was like a tsunami of depravity aimed at a mother who lived for her children. She was forced during a long and bitter Alaska winter to watch an entire school year go by without any knowledge of whether her children were even enrolled in school at all. Her home was devoid during that eight months of the sounds and excitement that make parenthood so enjoyable: the times watching movies or sitting down to dinner together. Birthdays, Christmas, the laughing, the playing, and the ability to guide a child through the everyday difficulties of life. As a result of the kidnappings, Emma was forced to cope with the idea that her four children were God-knows-where, if they were even alive, and who knows what Addis had told them. She was completely at Addis's mercy.

Over time, however, Emma repeatedly vowed to channel her anguish into action, and she relentlessly pursued law
enforcement to investigate. Her push to find her children
started to gain some momentum, like a train, slowly but
surely gathering steam, and the first big break for Emma
in her hunt was a local warrant sought by the Fairbanks
Police Department for Addis on four counts of custodial
interference. Because Addis was the subject of a federal
warrant for flight to avoid prosecution, the U.S. Attorney's
Office and the FBI got involved. With Emma helping, law
enforcement and volunteers distributed flyers and photos to
police departments across the country.

Eight months later, an exercise buff in Kalispell, Montana, started to think that a fellow gym-goer looked very
much like a man highlighted in a police flyer about four
abducted children from Alaska. The tipster had seen
Addis's picture on a flyer distributed in Kalispell and
called the local police department. Local police swooped
in on the gym, and Addis was arrested by local authorities.

The children were found minutes later locked in a
cabin Addis was keeping outside of Kalispell. They were
unharmed.

"I got a phone call in April of 1987," Emma would later
recall for a Las Vegas grand jury. "We flew to Montana and
picked them up."

The *Fairbanks Daily News-Miner* reported on the finding of the children in an April 1987 article. Emma told the
paper the capture of Addis by an alert witness "was just
one of those lucky moments."

"I just cried," Emma told the paper. "That's all I could
do. Right now I just want to thank everyone for their
prayers and concern."

Roger McCoy said a police investigation would later document the fact that, before moving the children to Montana, Addis had flown the children into a rural, remote cabin in British Columbia and stored them there for several months. A mug shot from Addis's arrest in Montana shows a shockingly different man in comparison to his time as a state trooper. He is sporting a thick beard and a flannel shirt and looks like he just emerged from the woods. He looks like an angry wild man. There is a truly wild look in his eyes.

"He had the kids stashed in a little cabin outside," Paul Bartlett said. "He would lock them in this place during the day, he would go to work, and he would come back at night. These poor kids—it was terrible. That went on for some period of time before they rounded him up and caught him."

Addis waived extradition and was flown back to Fairbanks. A grand jury was convened, and Emma, Addis's first wife; Sarah, his second wife; and his oldest daughter, Charlotte, recounted the ordeal. The young girl showed great bravery as she took the witness stand and told of her trip throughout Canada and the United States, winding up eventually in Montana. But first she told of Addis's attempted emotional manipulations of his children during their 1985 trip to Florida, when Addis was still married to Toni Martinez.

"He told us that he would like us to stay, and he was trying to convince us that we did not want to go back," Charlotte said. "He didn't want us to go back, and when we told him no, he got very angry."

Charlotte recalled how she and her siblings eventually called their mother and told her they didn't want to return to Alaska. Charlotte said they'd been forced to do so.

"I'd wanted him to come up to Fairbanks [the following summer, in 1986] and visit up there," Charlotte said. "He said that would be too expensive for him to come up, and that it would be a lot more economical for us to go down to Florida with him, and that he thought my mother didn't want . . . him to come up there. That he would get in trouble."

She recounted flying to Chicago and meeting her father. He was very happy to see the children. He picked them up in Martinez's gray pickup with the camper shell.

"We stayed around in Chicago for a couple hours, and then we drove to my grandparents' house in Michigan," Charlotte said. "And then we stayed a couple of days in Michigan, visited some relatives, and then we drove up to upper Michigan. He said . . . we were going to go sightseeing [in] Upper Michigan and Canada."

Addis drove the children from Canada to Montana. There, Charlotte said, her father bought a cabin and told the children "we were staying with him." Charlotte described the cabin as "accessible by horseback or car, four-wheel drive." Addis didn't register the children for school, saying it was "too late," and in the coming months, Addis rarely took the children into Kalispell. He warned the children to never call their mother again because he'd end up in jail.

"He said that he would get in a lot of trouble, and that we would probably never see him again," Charlotte recalled.

The children knew something was terribly wrong. They were in a difficult bind. They loved their father; they did not want to see him go to jail. But they also knew that something was definitely wrong. They agreed to wait and see what happened and hope someone would eventually figure out what was going on. They dreamed of being reunited with their mother but did not dare call her. They feared what might happen.

"He said she would probably forget [about] looking for us by Christmas or New Year's," Charlotte said.

On April 20, 1987, the police swooped into the cabin and rescued the kids. A grand jury indicted Addis on four counts of custodial interference, alleging Addis took the children "knowing he had no legal right to do so, and caused them to be removed from the state with intent to hold them for a protracted period." A lot of legal wrangling followed. Addis at one point tried to have his public defender, Paul Carnarski, removed from the case.

"I got a second opinion from a number of other legal representatives who felt that I had been charged with a crime I did not commit," Addis wrote in one court document. "I approached Mr. Carnarski and asked him to talk to the district attorney on my behalf; and inquire into the matter. This approach was made through another attorney. He failed to bring up the points I asked him to and, as a result, my situation became more tenuous by reducing the likelihood of a compromise."

Addis seemed to be in denial about being caught red-handed with the kids. The case seemed to be open-and-shut to just about everyone else. The order from the court had been clear: Addis was to buy round-trip tickets and get the kids back to Fairbanks by September. Instead, he'd stolen them and whisked them off to the Montana wilderness and told them they were not allowed to call their mother because he'd end up in prison. It was clear to everyone that Addis knew what he was doing and that if he got caught he was going to be arrested. In the fall of 1987, Addis agreed to plead guilty to a felony charge of custodial interference.

The judge in the case, Richard Savell, noted the meanness of the crime as he handed down the sentence, citing a mental health report that found Addis seemed to show very little remorse for his cruel behavior:

"The court, obviously, has to consider a number of factors in trying to fashion an appropriate sentence," Savell said. "The court has no doubt that the offense was committed out of love for Mr. Addis's children—a misguided love. The court does view this as an assault, in a figurative sense. It is an assault upon the family, it is an assault upon the children, it is an assault upon Mr. Addis's ex-wife, and it is an assault upon the legal institution which governed his behavior or governed the relationship between those children. Notwithstanding the difficulties Mr. Addis faced by his location out of the state of Alaska, and notwithstanding the difficulties in obtaining visitation of a type that would satisfy his needs, what he did, of his own unilateral wish, was to not place his wife or ex-wife in the same situation he had been in, but, rather, was to strip her of access to the children, and even more importantly, to strip the children of their mother, imposing upon them the guilt, the responsibility, and the injury of having them perceive themselves responsible for any change in the status quo, any reporting of the condition.

"It is troubling," the judge said. "I see [the results] of the mental health exam . . . and the court is concerned by many comments attributed to Mr. Addis. He's caused some undue stress to Emma. Well, that's putting it mildly. He doesn't think the children have been seriously harmed. That continues with the attached skepticism toward protests, opinions, or attempts at control by his ex-wife. The greatest harm Mr. Addis has at least expressed is to himself, to his sister, to his parents, because they don't have access to the children. Mr. Addis's affidavit says he believed the court order gave the children the right to choose to be with him and therefore he was doing no wrong. That is nonsense.

"That pronouncement was also belied by the fact that the children were given a different name when they were in Montana," the judge said. "It is belied by the fact that they were not permitted to call their mother and [were hidden away] for approximately eight months. If Mr. Addis believed he had the sanctity of the court's approval, he wouldn't have behaved in this fashion. I don't believe the children chose to live with him in September 1986. Addis violated the known order of the court. The court believes he intimidated the children or, at the very least, tried to influence them. The representation of the round-trip ticket was fraudulent on his part [and] the most innocent way of viewing it is that he was still playing games with the court, lying to the court and lying to Emma, but that he was doing that as a manipulation . . . that's the nicest way of viewing it.

"He says he panicked in September and intended to correct the matter but never did," the judge said. "And, there's nothing before the court to indicate that he would not still be living in Kalispell had he not been found. This is among the most serious of offenses. It's a continuing violation, that it lasted eight months and was perpetuated and re-perpetuated every day. In some ways, Mr. Addis's prior profession as a law enforcement officer gave him added expertise, or willpower, or inner strength, but also comes to haunt him now because this is a situation where, of all people—having served as a law enforcement officer—he should know that people cannot take the law into their own hands. The court believes it was a form of mental torture even if on a day-to-day basis they were well cared for and even became used to the form of captivity they faced. This kind of act must be condemned. Deterrence of others is a factor. The court fears that, if given the opportunity, he'd do it again in a minute."

The judge closed by saying that simply to trust Addis "is to be deceived." The former state trooper was committed, on November 2, 1987, to four years in state prison, with two and one half years suspended, meaning he would serve eighteen months in the Alaska Department of Corrections. It was a truly disgraceful moment for a man who had once worn the badge. The very public downfall and dispatch of Addis to prison indicated to everyone that Addis was a man who was thinking and acting like a criminal—not a cop.

"He [now seemed to be] one of those people who enjoyed thinking, 'I'm so good that I know how to get away with things,'" said Alaska judge Jane Kauvar of the public perception of Addis after the trial. "A pretty controlling character."

None of his former colleagues wanted anything to do with him at all. His arrest and sentencing to prison were a complete disgrace. None of his former state trooper friends ever visited him in prison. He had disgraced himself and brought dishonor on the state troopers. Addis had, in their eyes, flipped to the dark side, and his acts of torment toward his ex-wife were profoundly disturbing and deeply troubling.

"It was shameful," Jim McCann said. "When he came back, none of us went to visit him."

John Patrick Addis was now a convicted felon and very cruel criminal who'd put his ex-wife through eight months of hell. His former friends were left to wonder how it was even possible. He was a once-respected state trooper now acting like a crazy person and sentenced to serve hard time.

"It was like we'd never even known him," Gail McCann said. "It was like a Jekyll and Hyde–type individual. There was no indication about something like this."

Gail and Jim McCann, in describing Addis, frequently reference the title of the bestselling Ann Rule true-crime book *The Stranger Beside Me*, which chronicles Rule's real-life experience working next to serial killer Ted Bundy and not having any idea he was anything other than a sweet, nice young man. McCann, who read the book, said he had the exact same experience working with Addis and then seeing him morph into a complete stranger—a man capable of kidnapping his own kids and fleeing the state with no regard or concern for the impact the crime would have on the children or their mother.

"It was like we didn't even know him," Jim McCann said.

Emma has not discussed publicly how the kidnappings impacted the children in the long run. The McCanns and Paul Bartlett each said that, despite the trauma, John Addis's four children have grown into fine young women and men, and they live and work in Alaska to this day.

10 ... CAPE CORAL

There are no indications in the public record that John Patrick Addis was anything but a model inmate while serving time in Alaska. He was paroled from prison in 1988. He was allowed to leave the state of Alaska, and he moved to Fresno, California, on October 18 that same year in what is known as an interstate compact agreement. Alaska agreed to let Addis move to California on parole, but he would be required to report to a California parole officer there. Law enforcement records indicate he met a woman in the Fresno area, moved in with her, got engaged to her, then stole her money and disappeared. The theft of money was apparently not reported to police locally, and investigators would only become aware of it years after the fact. Addis officially stopped reporting to parole officers in Fresno in March 1989. Instead of issuing an absconder warrant, the state of California, strangely, simply closed the case. The state of Alaska, however, was not so kind.

Records with the Alaska Department of Corrections indicate that Addis was the subject of a statewide absconder
warrant issued by the Fairbanks Department of Parole, but
Addis would never be arrested on this warrant. In fact, it
seemed very few people, if anyone, were interested in following up on or tracking down the Alaska state trooper
gone bad once he got out of jail and failed to report to his
parole officer.

According to an assemblage of law enforcement records,
what followed next was a remarkable journey by John Patrick Addis across the United States and back. His whereabouts were documented in at least seven different states
by police or witness accounts after he disappeared from his
parole agent's radar screen in Fresno in 1989. Sometimes
he used his real name. Sometimes he used aliases. The
states Addis was definitely in include Arizona, Michigan,
New Mexico, Washington, Utah, Georgia, and Florida.

There was a consistent pattern in much of Addis's travels across America, according to police records. He was
constantly working out at gyms, and he regularly took
jobs as a fitness instructor. He also, according to police
records, was constantly soliciting women while working as
a fitness instructor. In several instances, he dated women
he met at the gym. He would tell them he loved them. He
would woo them with his good looks and charm. Often,
the women thought they'd stumbled across their dream
man. He was a good-looking, blond-haired, green-eyed fitness professional who would move in with them, tell them
he loved them, then abruptly disappear with their money,
leaving them with empty promises of marriage and shat-
tered hearts.

The police records clearly place Addis in Cape Coral,

Florida, in the early 1990s. It is a beautiful resort community and region that is home to more than half a million people, and Addis claimed, in a résumé later collected by police, that he had lived in Cape Coral from 1983 to 1990. The résumé later proved to be filled with lies and false addresses, but, nonetheless, Addis stated he had extensive ties to the Cape Coral region. Addis would claim repeatedly that he'd been a fitness instructor for years in the southwest corner of the Sunshine State.

Addis, while living in Florida, also crafted a new persona under a new alias. He was no longer former Alaska state trooper John Addis. Now, he was well-traveled fitness expert and personal trainer John L. Edwards. Police reports indicate "John Edwards" was actually a real person who lived in Cape Coral, Florida, and Addis had somehow obtained the man's driver's license. It is believed he may have stolen the man's license out of a gym locker or car. Addis then used the information to obtain a duplicate, fraudulent driver's license under the name John L. Edwards. Addis then created a whole new persona and lengthy professional résumé under the John L. Edwards identity. While living as John L. Edwards, he told people that he'd gotten a bachelor's degree in physiology from Michigan State, or sometimes, he said Michigan Technological University, the latter of which is located in the far western reaches of Michigan's Upper Peninsula.

Addis, living as John L. Edwards, bragged of taking numerous human biology and physiology classes at the postgraduate level. Living under this fictitious identity, he talked freely about his entire life as John L. Edwards. A résumé he wrote under the name said, "I have a passion for learning. [I've taken] classes [in] immunology, cardiology, histology, serology, pathology, and medical endocrinology."

Addis said he was a fitness instructor who also happened to be a master salesman. He said he had a special knack for getting visitors to the gym signed up as new members and he often convinced those members to pay for personalized fitness instructions from Addis at the gyms where he worked. He said he'd studied the techniques of sales guru Tom Hopkins and had taken Hopkins's seminar "The Art of Selling" along with numerous other "sales, health and fitness seminars."

Addis falsely claimed on his John L. Edwards résumé that from 1983 to 1990—a period of time that included the eighteen months Addis spent in prison in Alaska—he was the "owner of Advanced Athletics," a fitness business in Cape Coral, Florida. He listed a false address for Advanced Athletics, which offered as a product "all levels of sales and marketing for training systems dedicated primarily to tennis and swim strengthening."

On the same résumé, Addis claimed he'd been a fitness instructor from 1984 to 1990 at another gym, Body Physique of Fort Myers, which is just across the river from Cape Coral. In addition, Addis said on his résumé that in the early 1990s he owned and operated yet another fitness business, called Advanced Training Systems. He listed a fake address for this business in Cape Coral, Florida, noting the Advanced Training Systems business involved "all levels of sales and marketing for training systems dedicated to the general population, i.e., athletes, executives and housewives."

"Training included general fitness, weight loss and

specific strength training programs," Addis noted on his résumé.

Addis, meanwhile, continued to be completely obsessive about fitness. He continued to lift a lot of weights and took nutritional supplements from a fitness nutrition company based in Cape Coral. The new John L. Edwards had emerged from prison touting himself as a fitness guru. He said he was an absolute expert on taking care of the human body, and he seemed committed to the fitness profession for life.

"I have owned and operated my own personal training business for more than 10 years," Addis wrote. "This is a highly competitive field, and I have been aggressive in club sales . . . introducing an average [of] 28 to 30 new members a month to fitness.

"[My] objective is to find a permanent position with a leading gym or health club in sales or marketing," Addis said. "I would prefer to relocate to the Southwest Mountain states. . . . I have a passion for Nordic skiing. Sales is important to me as this is a field I know I can excel in. I have no interest in management.

"The fitness industry is my life," Addis wrote. "There are only two kinds of people in the world. Those who work out and those who need to start a program. There is no excuse good enough to neglect your health."

On May 8, 1990, a woman named Jan Cornell, of Cape Coral, Florida, welcomed a new roommate, Lisa Story, into her condominium. Jan Cornell was a very attractive single mom who worked in the medical field. She had a promising, beautiful eleven-year-old blond-haired daughter named Robin. The child was the light of her life.

On May 10—two days after Story moved into the condominium—Jan Cornell tucked her daughter into bed. With Story home for the evening, Jan Cornell planned to head over to her boyfriend's house and watch some late-night television. It was a rare opportunity, for sure, for her to be able to get out and meet her boyfriend, and Story agreed to watch Robin for just a little bit. Jan Cornell was planning on being back in just a couple of hours.

What happened next in that condominium, that night, while Jan was gone, would be one of the most notorious and brutal crimes in Florida history.

Jan Cornell fell asleep on her boyfriend's couch. According to media accounts and a recap of the crime on the television show *America's Most Wanted*, Jan Cornell woke up in a panic at 4 a.m. She had to be at work at an area hospital in thirty minutes. She raced home to shower and get dressed. She arrived at the condominium and, curiously, found a bottom lock on the door to the condo locked. The other lock on the door was supposed to be locked—not this one.

"Jan had told both Robin and Lisa before she left the house not to lock it because it was broken and she wouldn't be able to get in the house," *America's Most Wanted* wrote in a summary of the case. "Jan knocked lightly on the front door and thought she heard footsteps coming down."

Jan Cornell then went to the rear of the condo and found a sliding-glass door wide open. Panic set in. She entered the home and found family photos in unusual places. They'd been taken off a wall and set out on display on an ironing board. This was bizarre, and she knew something was terribly wrong.

What she saw next, when she ran upstairs, was the most horrifying thing a parent could ever imagine. She found her daughter Robin's naked body on the floor in the bedroom. Police arrived, and Lisa Story, thirty-two, was found dead in her bed. Police conducted a massive investigation, concluding that a heartless killer had snuck into the condominium. He took a pillow and, with great strength, smothered Lisa Story to death. The killer used the pillow to kill young Robin as well. He then sexually assaulted both victims after death.

The killer was apparently expecting to be in the home alone the entire evening, but Jan Cornell may have startled him. There is speculation that Jan's unexpected arrival caused the killer to run off early.

It was a shocking crime given its heinousness. It was cold-blooded to the extreme, and the entire communities of Cape Coral and Fort Myers were outraged.

To this day, no killer has ever been arrested.

The crime scene offered some very valuable clues to detectives. Most importantly, the killer's bodily fluids were found at the crime scene. Police have a DNA profile of the killer and have eliminated more than seventy potential suspects through DNA testing.

There were some other intriguing clues. On a television, authorities found a set of keys that they now believe could have belonged to the killer and were left behind. *America's Most Wanted* has published on its website a widely disseminated public account of the crime in the hope it will generate new leads and clues in the case.

One of the keys on the keychain is described by police as fitting an older model Toyota. The police disseminated this list of possible models for the car key:

'78–'88 Corolla

'70–'89 Celica

'81–'90 Landcruiser

'85–'90 MR-2

'84–'89 Supra

'80–'90 Tercel

'71–'88 Toyota pickup truck

The Florida Department of Law Enforcement reports that a watch was stolen from the crime scene. The watch was a 1990 Seiko, with a white rectangular face with gold band. "To Randy, Happy Birthday, 5-11-90, All My Love, Lisa" was the inscription on the back of the watch. The Florida Department of Law Enforcement says the watch, Lisa Story's driver's license, and a credit card were stolen from the crime scene and have never been recovered.

A profile of the killer was crafted, according to *America's Most Wanted*. It was determined the offender was likely unknown to the victims, may be sexually inadequate, and may be physically strong.

Police have investigated the case time and again but have not been able to solve it. It has been a very frustrating homicide investigation for Cape Coral cops. The longtime lead detective in the case, Charlie Garrett, has appeared repeatedly on national television seeking help. The police department also brought in the Vidocq Society to investigate. These experts from law enforcement, science, and even artistic backgrounds volunteer their time to try and help solve cold cases.

"Maybe they'll see something we missed," Garrett told CNN in 2002.

The effort turned up no leads. The Cape Coral Police Department then hired a retired New York City homicide investigator, Fidel Balan, to review the case for a year to see if any new leads could be developed. He too was unable to crack the cold case.

On the nineteenth anniversary of the homicides, the Cape Coral police issued the following press release:

The Cape Coral Police Department continues to investigate the city's most visible unsolved homicides as the 19th anniversary approaches of the murders of Robin Cornell and Lisa Story. In a painful twist of timing, this year's anniversary falls on Mother's Day.

The murders have perplexed investigators since May 10, 1990, when an unknown assailant entered Jan Cornell's home and killed her 11-year-old daughter, Robin and Jan's new roommate, 32-year-old Lisa Story. Lisa had just moved in and had agreed to babysit with Robin while Jan visited her boyfriend the night before. Early that morning, Jan Cornell returned to her home at 631 SE 12th Avenue to find her daughter's naked body lying on the floor of her bedroom. Lisa's body also was found in her bed. Both victims were suffocated and sexually assaulted.

The double-homicide has been featured twice on *America's Most Wanted*, airing on January 21, 2006, and again on July 28, 2007. Two years ago, Cape Police hired a retired New York City detective, Fidel Balan, to investigate this cold case and try to develop any new leads on the murders. Balan was unable to solve the case prior to the expiration of his contract.

The Cape Police have not given up and are continuing the investigation. Two detectives in the Major Case Unit from the department's Investigative Services Bureau have been assigned the case. Detective Kurt Grau and Detective Christy Jo Ellis have been tasked with reviewing the case files and continuing to develop leads. The detectives remain optimistic even though a significant amount of time has passed since Robin and Lisa were killed. Several interviews have been conducted recently, and new theories are being explored.

Jan Cornell continues to hold out hope that her daughter's murder someday will be solved, and she supports the Cape Coral Police Department's steadfast determination to find the killer.

Jan Cornell told a Florida television station that she'd found a hero in John Walsh. Walsh's son, Adam, was murdered in Florida in 1981. Walsh founded *America's Most Wanted* afterward and has helped catch thousands of criminals through the television show. Walsh waited nearly two decades before learning who the killer of his young son was, and Jan Cornell said it was an inspirational story for her.

"[Cape Coral police] are committed to finding her killer," Jan Cornell told a television reporter. "[The police] know I'm not going anywhere. They know I'll go away when they call me and say, 'We have him.' Like John Walsh said, 'Don't give up. Do not give up.' "

A request in January 2010 to the Alaska Department of Corrections for some paperwork for this book turned up some interesting new information. They had in their possession just one page on Addis. There, printed in the file, was the following note:

> [On] 9/12/95, Detective Charlie Garrett of Cape Coral Fla., 813 574 0649, called to advise defendant [John Patrick Addis] is a suspect in a double homicide and the disappearance of a female.

An e-mail to Jim McCann, the former Alaska homicide investigator, about the note in the Alaska corrections file saying Addis was a suspect in a double murder in Cape Coral revealed that McCann recalled having heard about the case. McCann had offered to help any law enforcement agencies that ever investigated Addis because he's thoroughly dismayed at the criminality of his former friend. In fact, as Addis was rampaging his way through the country, committing crimes, McCann contemplated whether he should personally get involved in the investigation of Addis. He believed John Addis, given his background and mental instability, was a truly dangerous individual.

He recalls talking to a Florida detective years ago about the matter. The detective indicated Addis was a suspect in the murders of a woman and girl in Florida. McCann remembered the detective telling him there was a random connection between the child victim's mother and Addis.

The connection was that they both went to the same gym.

"As to the Florida case . . . what I was told by a detective those many years ago was that 'John Edwards' had worked at the same gym one or both of the victims worked out at," McCann said.

McCann remembered some other very specific details about the Florida case.

"I know exactly about the Florida case," McCann said. "It was a nurse and her daughter, and [the] mom went to the same gym 'John Edwards' was employed at. I forgot about it being Florida, but I did mention it to you. After I'd run the lead down and spoke with the detective, I was sure John Addis had done the crimes, or at least as sure as I could be in my position."

Charlie Garrett, the detective who called the Alaska Department of Corrections fifteen years ago and termed Addis a suspect in a "double homicide," was the detective in charge of the investigation of the murder of Lisa Story and Robin Cornell.

In the decades after the Cornell and Story murders, Addis would go on to be linked to four other killings. Usually, the epicenter of his criminal endeavors revolved around his ability to meet women at fitness centers, which made him a likely suspect in the Cape Coral slayings.

The name John Addis was not a name that was immediately familiar to Cape Coral police, but when presented with his previous criminal history and background, Cape Coral detectives took the information seriously. With no new leads in a twenty-year-old case, they are going to try and rule John Patrick Addis out as the killer of Robin Cornell and Lisa Story. Detective Kurt Grau said they'll be checking their old, archived case files to discern if there was, in fact, a connection between Addis, a man named John L. Edwards, and any of the victims.

"We are definitely going to look into him," Grau said. "We are willing to try anything; after twenty years, any new info is good."

11 . . . ALIENS

John Patrick Addis was a full-fledged believer in alien life. He told many people there was evidence that aliens once mated with humans and that their offspring was the Caucasian race, and he believed one could go to the American Southwest and witness alien aircraft in the sky and listen to alien transmissions over the radio. The U.S. government, he believed, was covering up the presence of alien life. He also believed in many of the more commonly espoused threads in alien theory in America—that the triangle-like pattern of ancient temples constructed in Guatemala was no accident. It was similar to a pattern observed on the moon. Stonehenge, he believed, was likely constructed with the help of aliens. The pyramids in Egypt were at the exact center of longitude and latitude and had to be constructed with the help of aliens from the heavens. These pyramids were a sign from the heavens. The same could be said for the pyramids and temples in the jungles of Mexico and Guatemala as well as the remarkable stone-work monuments pieced together in the highlands of Bolivia. There was simply no way ancient man could have built these monuments of granite and diorite rock without machinery brought to earth by aliens.

In 1990, Alaska state trooper Roger McCoy received a call from his sister-in-law, Emma. Emma informed him that there had been a bizarre development: John Patrick Addis's airplane had been found on a rural, federal airstrip in Selma, Alabama. Emma told her brother-in-law that she needed help retrieving the plane because the feds had called and wanted her to come pick up the aircraft. Roger McCoy found it unusual that John Addis would abandon his cherished plane like that.

"It was a Cessna . . . and he'd flown it into Selma and abandoned it," McCoy said. "[Emma told me], 'They can't find John. He's on the lam for something he did in Florida.'"

McCoy said it was not clear what Addis had done in Florida or why he was wanted. He nonetheless agreed to fly to Selma and pick up the aircraft. McCoy was greeted by Alabama law enforcement, and the Alabama officers told him they suspected Addis was involved in narcotics trafficking, running shipments of narcotics into the United States.

"I went down there and checked the plane out, and they said, 'This guy is running drugs,'" McCoy said. "'Whoever had it is running drugs' [and] I think it was the Alabama state police who told me this aircraft was a suspect vehicle used in drug trafficking from either Colombia or Cuba."

McCoy was surprised at the development. McCoy had not previously envisioned his former friend as a narco-trafficker. McCoy could see, however, Addis being able to pull off such a crime because of his willingness to take huge risks while flying. McCoy had been a personal witness to Addis's daring piloting, which is what it would have taken to fly from South America or the Caribbean into Alabama to deliver drugs. The incident further convinced McCoy that Addis was now completely off the deep end, and it saddened him because Addis had been a man with such great potential. He was incredibly smart and a hard worker with a beautiful woman for a wife and four splendid children, but that life was a memory now. The John Addis who kidnapped his kids, went to prison and then failed to report to parole, and abandoned a plane in Alabama was not the man McCoy had known from the Alaska State Trooper barracks.

Meanwhile, Emma continued to deal with the aftermath of her ex-husband's bizarre behavior. She would learn after her divorce that Addis had performed a fraudulent paperwork transaction against his own daughter involving the Cessna found in Florida. The aircraft was the subject of a fraudulent aircraft bill of sale. Addis, it appeared, had listed his fifteen-year-old daughter as the owner of his airplane, and he'd produced the fake aircraft bill of sale to make it look like he'd purchased the aircraft from Charlotte. This, in turn, apparently caused Emma a string of headaches. Emma, through her Alaska attorney, James D. Nordale, filed a document known as a "complaint to cancel

a forged instrument" in the Alaska state courts to clear up
the matter.

The document reads as follows:

> Comes now, the plaintiff, by and through her under-
> signed counsel, and hereby complains and alleges as
> follows:
>
> Plaintiff is the mother of Charlotte Addis and brings
> this action for and on behalf of her daughter. Both plain-
> tiff and her daughter are residents of the state of Alaska.
> Defendant John P. Addis is believed to be a resident of the
> state of California. Charlotte Addis is the owner of and
> has constructive possession of that certain Cessna 185D,
> registration # N1559F. John Addis claims the [aircraft
> bill of sale] purports to convey the aircraft from Char-
> lotte Addis to John Addis. Charlotte Addis, [however],
> never executed this bill of sale or any other bill of sale
> conveying said aircraft to defendant or any other person,
> and the bill of sale is false, fraudulent, and forged.

Addis, now missing after being released from prison
and absconding from parole, never responded to the complaint. Alaska judge Jane Kauvar approved the request by
Emma's attorney.

"Very strange," Kauvar said of the idea of Addis forging
his own daughter's name on a fraudulent document.

John Patrick Addis moved from state to state in the
following years, working at fitness centers and gyms at
almost every stop along the way. He befriended multiple
women, moved in with them, ripped them off and disappeared. Shortly after leaving Florida, Addis met a woman
named Susan Friedman* in Arizona in 1990. She was,

according to Las Vegas police reports, employed at a local bank and met Addis while working out at a gym. She must have fallen in love with Addis very quickly because court records with the state of Arizona indicate the couple was issued a marriage license in late 1990. According to police records, the couple briefly lived together in Tustin, in Orange County, California, before Friedman divorced Addis for unknown reasons. The two, however, remained in contact for two more years, according to Las Vegas police reports. Further details of the relationship and their contacts with one another remain a mystery because Friedman, now living in Canada, refused to say anything about Addis at all when contacted by the Canadian Mounties on behalf of Las Vegas investigators who would later attempt to track Addis's whereabouts throughout the country.

Las Vegas police would also conclude Addis spent at least some time in Georgia in 1989 and Oklahoma in 1990. He claimed to be in Florida and Arizona that same year, Canada a year later, and, in 1993, he was back in Florida for a brief stop, where he bought a blue pickup truck in the Orlando area before moving on to Salt Lake City. He remained there until 1994. Addis became a suspect but was never arrested in the theft of some two hundred dollars in cash, credit cards, and a driver's license from a Salt Lake resident named Creighton Chun. Chun reported to police that his cash, credit cards, and license were stolen from his car while it was parked at a baseball diamond in the city. Years later, Chun's documentation was recovered in Addis's belongings by police.

Salt Lake City is also the place where Addis, posing as John L. Edwards, met Sandra Felix*—a charming, petite, modest country girl originally from Texas. She, too, met Addis at the gym where he was working as a fitness instructor. Las Vegas police, with the assistance of Salt Lake City detectives, would later investigate Addis's relationship with Felix. She, like the other women in Addis's life, told police she at first found Addis to be charming, handsome, and loving. He was incredibly good-looking and fit. He lifted weights every other day and consumed nutritional supplements from a Cape Coral, Florida, company called Advanced Body Dynamics. Addis told Felix he did not have any children and had never been married. Felix concluded she'd hit the jackpot as far as men are concerned. John had no baggage whatsoever.

Addis soon told Felix he wanted to get married and settle down in Salt Lake. He wanted to have a family. He also told her that when he married her, he would take her last name, Felix, and abandon his name of Edwards, which she found completely strange.

"Felix said Addis wanted her to marry him, and suggested that when they did marry, he would take her last name as opposed to her taking his," Las Vegas police would write later in police reports documenting Addis's multiple incidents of fleecing women. "Felix found this a little strange but Addis acted as if he were not serious and it was not discussed further."

Felix would also reveal a couple of interesting details about Addis to police. He was, she said, consumed with worshipping the ancient Egyptian sun god Ra: the ruler of both the natural earth and the underworld. He paid homage to the sun and its powers. Felix said Addis was also obsessed and consumed with aliens, extraterrestrials, and unidentified flying objects, or UFOs. He revealed to her that he'd been to New Mexico, Arizona, and Nevada to investigate UFO sightings. He truly believed they were real, she said. Addis was convinced that thousands of years ago human beings had mated with aliens, and there would come a time, Addis said, when aliens would arrive on earth in spaceships and bring their human children back home to an alien world, millions of miles away in another galaxy.

"Felix said Addis was fanatical about the presence of extraterrestrials," police reports state. "[He believed there had been a] government cover-up of an alien presence. In fact, he'd written a screenplay about it called *Purposeful Deceit*."

Felix told authorities that Addis's screenplay, *Purposeful Deceit*, was about alien abductions throughout the United States. Addis, she said, shopped the screenplay about alien abductions to Hollywood producers. He was rejected by Castle Rock Entertainment in Beverly Hills and others and received a steady stream of rejection slips.

Felix and Addis were preparing to marry in the fall of 1994 when he simply picked up and disappeared. She checked her bank account the day after he left and found hundreds of dollars missing. She went to the gym where Addis worked and learned Addis was suspected of stealing fifteen hundred dollars from the gym. The incident was not reported to police "due to a lack of evidence." Felix was devastated to learn Addis was last seen driving south, out of Utah, in a beige pickup truck. His route south on Interstate 15 would take him on a direct path to the Utah-Nevada border and eventually to Las Vegas.

Devastated and heartbroken, Felix eventually left Salt Lake and headed back to Texas.

In early 1995, Shannon Lyndon was working out at a Las Vegas gym called Family Fitness on Eastern Avenue, roughly two miles east of the Las Vegas Strip, when she met a fitness instructor named John Edwards. Lyndon, a Las Vegas resident, is a stunning woman. She is incredibly attractive, with a beautiful figure and an even more wonderful personality. She keeps herself in good shape and works out at the gym quite frequently. Edwards approached her at the gym and started making small talk, introducing himself as John Edwards. She noticed he was big, muscular, and in very good shape. He had a handsome face, and he told her he was a writer. He said he'd written a screenplay about alien abductions called *Purposeful Deceit*.

"He asked me if I wanted to be in a movie based on the screenplay," Lyndon would tell authorities later in a quote paraphrased by police. "I considered it a sexual advance and didn't accept his offer."

Lyndon thought the request was a little strange, but she didn't think anything more of it at the time.

Another woman, Nina Lebanon, had a similar experience in 1995 with a fitness instructor who introduced himself to her as John Edwards at the now defunct Q Club gym in northwest Las Vegas. John Edwards was the one who welcomed her into the gym, gave her a guided tour, and asked her to fill out an interest card at the gym, meaning she was considering joining.

Lebanon didn't join the gym but was surprised to get a call from John Edwards at home the following day. He continued to call her at home and at work several times after that, and she found the advances creepy.

"He apparently had taken her phone number from an interest card [at the gym] and began calling her at home, and at work, in an effort to have her read a screenplay that he had written, and possibly appear in a future movie production," police wrote after interviewing Lebanon. "Lebanon did not follow through with Edwards' offer."

Yet another attractive woman, Cindi Middlebury,* met John Edwards at a Las Vegas gym in 1995. She did not immediately sense anything wrong with him, and she was attracted to him because he was very handsome and well built. He was, like her, into physical fitness. He told her he'd been through some abusive relationships, and she was surprised at this. John Edwards seemed like a very loving man to her, and she thought she was falling in love with him after only a couple of weeks of dating.

Alarm bells went off, however, in Middlebury's mind while watching a television show about aliens at a home in Las Vegas where John Edwards was renting a room. The show focused on the possibility of extraterrestrial life. And during the show, it seemed to her that Edwards transformed into a completely different person. He started ranting about alien life. He believed aliens had mated with humans hundreds of years ago and would one day return to earth to gather up their offspring. Middlebury noticed Edwards's appearance completely changed when he started talking about aliens. He became frantic and angry as she questioned whether he was serious. He said he was, and he became very upset.

"Edwards became very upset about the government's cover-up of the alien presence and [he] spoke of building bombs and attacking the government," Middlebury would later say in a quote paraphrased by police.

Middlebury was frightened. She waited until Edwards went to sleep and started scurrying through his personal belongings. In a duffle bag she found multiple licenses and IDs of the man she knew as John Edwards. Each identity had Edwards's photo on it but a different name. There were at least six different aliases and fake identifications.

Middlebury was terrified by the development. She left a note saying the relationship was over and left the house immediately. Edwards called her repeatedly in the following days. She told him if he continued to call her, she would contact the police.

She never heard from him again.

12 ... FRIENDS

Tara Rivera is a New York City girl at heart. She was born and raised in Queens, and although she's lived in Las Vegas for more than two decades now, the thick New York accent and feistiness still linger. She's a sweet, pretty, colorful, five-feet-one fireplug. Now married with two children, she wisecracks that "she likes Latin men," like her longtime husband, who himself is a handsome former New Yorker. There are a lot of Las Vegans like Tara: former New York State residents who have relocated from the Big Apple and upstate and the cold winter weather to Sin City, its sun, and the edginess of the city that can be found nowhere else. Tara has lived in Las Vegas through the city's good and bad of the last twenty-two years.

When she first came to Vegas, houses were astonishingly cheap, and the city still felt relatively small. Over the following fifteen years, the city boomed, and hundreds of thousands of people migrated there in search of a new beginning. A new start. She's watched as the city's traffic increased and the crime increased. Rivera says if she had it to do over again, "knowing what I know now," she's not sure she would have ever come here, but Las Vegas is now her home for good. She loves the city despite all the ups and downs, the traffic, and the crime. Despite the drawbacks, it's still a great city, and like New York, it's a city that will be in her heart forever.

In 1995 Rivera was working at the MGM Grand casino. This was the time when the MGM truly was the cornerstone of the city gaming mecca. The gargantuan, glass-covered complex at the corner of Tropicana and Las Vegas Boulevard was, in the 1990s, the hottest spot in town. It was where the once great boxer Mike Tyson steamrolled through lesser opponents, punished them with powerful, furious punches, drawing crowds of rappers, the rich, and the wannabes. The MGM was the premier gambling spot for high rollers from across the globe, and they dumped hundreds of thousands of dollars into the mega casino's coffers.

Rivera's job at the MGM was in telecommunications. She was responsible for booking tourists into room-and-show reservations over the phone. It was a fun job. And while doing it, she met a co-worker who would become a very dear friend. Joann Albanese, a divorced mother of two daughters, was spunky, witty, and fun.

"She was very, very witty, funny, and she had a great personality," Rivera said. "We just clicked right away and we became very, very close.

"Joann was adorable," Rivera said. "She had fluffy, above-the-shoulder . . . hair. Very curly, fluffy, and adorable. She was very spoiled [by her ex-husband], and we were great friends. We talked every day."

Rivera met Joann's daughters, Amber and Brittany, and found them to be very beautiful girls. She knew the three were very close. Rivera described Joann as a "wonderful mother." In fact, she was an incredibly doting mother. Joann was elegant and always very well kept. She liked to be pampered, and Rivera described her good friend as a woman used to the finer things in life.

"We went to New York, we stayed at the Grand Hyatt, and this is what she was used to," Rivera said. "We had a beautiful hotel room, and everything was perfect. She was used to nice accommodations."

Joann was also fanatic about organization and having a clean house. Joann was organized to the max. A clean freak. She had to have everything in just the right place at her home in the upscale Lakes community of northwest Las Vegas.

"Her home, cleaning, everything had to be perfect," Rivera said. "She had certain things that had to be a certain way. [When she traveled], she was a stickler for packing like a week before. She would have at least two or three suitcases. Stuff that she didn't even need, she would bring. Everything had to be perfectly in place. Everything had to be done: her hair, her nails, everything."

Joann was also a woman with a temper and was "feisty, like me," Rivera said.

Rivera described Tom Albanese as a warm, friendly, and very decent man. Rivera said Joann had been divorced for a couple of years by the time she met her, and Joann struggled through a couple of short-term relationships with men after the failure of the marriage that produced her two children.

"Joann and her daughters were very close, and I think there were some rebellion issues surfacing [with her older daughter]," Rivera said. "She was the disciplinarian [of the family], and she's the one who held it all together."

Brenda Ulrich knew Joann Albanese from when she was a very young woman. Joann went to Western High School in Las Vegas, which is the same high school Brenda's husband graduated from.

"I went to Bonanza High School [in Las Vegas], and I've lived here since I was three years old," Ulrich said. "My husband and I have been married for thirty years, and [Joann and I had] stayed in contact and been friends all through our adult lives. [Joann] became one of my best friends."

Another longtime Las Vegan who knew Joann very well was Eli Koch. Koch was born in Brazil, but her parents were German. Joann's mother, Margarete, was originally from Germany, and her father served in World War II, so Joann and Eli could relate to one another very well.

"I tell you, Joann was one of my best friends," Koch said. "I got a chance to laugh and joke with her regularly. She was very simple. We used to talk a little bit about that she and her mother used to speak strictly German. Fluent."

Brenda Ulrich thought the world of Joann Albanese and her sister, Dollie Greenrock Wells. Joann was tough and sweet. She was a loving wife and mother to her two young daughters. Joann, Ulrich said, had a fiery personality at times and could be a little explosive when she saw something she didn't like. She wouldn't hold back if something was bothering her. She would tell you, in no uncertain terms, how she felt whether or not you were going to like what she had to say.

"She was a fun lady," Ulrich said. "She was compassionate, loving and crazy, all at the same time. She cared about people. She had a temper, too."

Ulrich knew Joann's ex-husband, too. She, like others, said Tom Albanese is a top-notch person and father who treated his wife and children very well. The couple spoiled their children in Las Vegas because they were able to, because of Tom Albanese's success as a food broker in Vegas. Both parents lavished the kids with love and the family traveled a lot. Tom, Ulrich said, treated Joann with great respect and tried to provide her with everything she wished for.

Joann, Ulrich said, would often send her notes or cards in the mail thanking her for her friendship.

"The last card I got from her was when I quit smoking," Ulrich said. "It was a silly little card she sent in the mail, and it said, 'Go ahead and tell everyone you quit smoking so when you start up again, you'll look like an idiot!' She had a sense of humor."

Koch came to know the Albanese family because Tom Albanese and Koch's husband were both in the food distribution business.

"Tom Albanese and Joann are both very, very nice people," Koch said. "My husband used to be in the food business . . . and since Tom Albanese was a food broker . . . we used to go to Hawaii and Mexico for company conventions, and we always used to go together [as families]. When we traveled, the guys would go off [their] own way and play golf, and the ladies used to go shopping. We'd go to their house for the holidays. Sometimes [Tom and Joann] used to take long trips, and I used to take care of their [daughters], Amber and Brittany. Very lovely girls." Koch thought Tom Albanese and Joann were the perfect couple. Koch remembers learning that they were divorcing in 1991, and she was completely stunned. The couple broke the news to her and her husband during a couples dinner in Las Vegas.

"They'd invited us to a gourmet dinner at a new Chinese restaurant [in northwest Las Vegas], and we met there and had a good time," Koch said. "All of a sudden, they each said, 'This is our good-bye dinner.' I was like, 'What do you mean?' They said, 'Because we are getting divorced.' [I was very sad about it] because they were each so nice, so sweet, and so peaceful. I really don't know why [they divorced]."

Ulrich, too, was surprised by the divorce. Joann, she said, started dating again in the years after the divorce, and she wanted to eventually remarry and rebuild her life with a new man. One man she dated was the Ulrichs' friend David Kartin,* but the relationship eventually faltered. Later, Kartin married another woman, and he asked Ulrich's husband to be his best man. This prompted Joann's temper to flare big-time. Ulrich was saddened when Joann showed up at her front door, yelling about how Ulrich's husband could consider being Kartin's best man.

"She came to my house and was very upset and felt betrayed," Ulrich said. "Yelling and screaming. I think she just felt betrayed."

Ulrich wasn't happy with the incident and what she felt was Joann's unnecessary display of anger. As a result she and Joann stopped talking for a while. As time passed, though, Ulrich tried to reach out to Joann and repair the friendship. She and Joann were good friends, and it pained Ulrich to know that such a minor issue had caused her to lose contact with her dear friend.

"I called her and left a message on her voice recorder," Ulrich said. "I said, 'I really want our friendship to continue.' I never heard back from her, and the next thing I knew, I [saw Joann's picture] on the news, and it was devastating."

Alaska state trooper John Patrick Addis is pictured in a passport photo from 1983, shortly before he abruptly resigned from Alaska law enforcement.
Photo from Las Vegas police files

John Patrick Addis is pictured in Alaska in an undated photo gathered as evidence by Las Vegas police.
Photo from Las Vegas police files

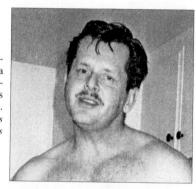

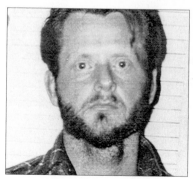

John Patrick Addis is pictured shortly after his arrest in Montana on charges he kidnapped his four children.
Photo from Las Vegas police files

Joann Albanese is pictured in her travel agent identification card found in her purse after her disappearance.
Photo from Las Vegas grand jury evidence vault

International Airlines Travel Agent Network

ASTA American Society of Travel Agents
Integrity in Travel

ID TRAVEL AGENT CARD

AAFFORDABLE LAS VEGAS
LAS VEGAS NV US
29-7 9747 1
JOANN ALBANESE
ALB5 6J01 2051 E11
1094/94 03/96
SERVICE DATE VALID TO
IATA 0892960690

Employee
Spouse
Joann
Albanese

Joann Albanese is pictured in what appears to be a gym identification card.
Photo from Las Vegas grand jury evidence vault

This photograph of "John Edwards" and Joann Albanese was taken by an unidentified tourist during the couple's trip to Hawaii in 1995. Joann had no idea at the time that "Edwards" was actually John Addis, and this photo later appeared in countless wanted posters for Addis after Albanese's disappearance from Las Vegas. *Photo from Las Vegas grand jury evidence vault*

When Las Vegas police searched the room of "John Edwards" in Las Vegas, they found identifications and credit cards of another man stolen from a vehicle in Utah. *Photo from Las Vegas grand jury evidence vault*

Multiple identifications of "John Edwards" were found in his belongings in Las Vegas after he disappeared with his girlfriend of four months, Joann Albanese. *Photo from Las Vegas grand jury evidence vault*

Another alias Addis frequently used was J. Charles Peterson, which is a name he adopted in both Florida and Mexico. *Photo from Las Vegas police files*

A truck left in Las Vegas by "John Edwards" after the disappearance of Joann Albanese is depicted in the Las Vegas police tow yard. Authorities had great difficulty in tracing the ownership of the vehicle. *Photo from Las Vegas grand jury evidence vault*

A roll of brown packing tape was found on the counter in Joann Albanese's bathroom after her disappearance. This photo depicts the tape as it was found by police. *Photo from Las Vegas grand jury evidence vault*

Joann Albanese's gold Honda was found abandoned in Little Hell's Canyon, Arizona, in 1995.   *Photo from Las Vegas grand jury evidence vault*

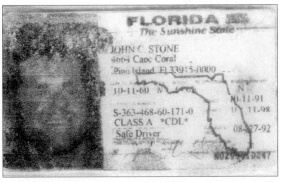

One of the many aliases John Patrick Addis used during his North American crime spree was that of John C. Stone, as is indicated on this fake Florida driver's license.   *Photo from Las Vegas police files*

Las Vegas police Detective Larry Hanna spent more than a decade trying to solve the killing of Joann Albanese and was at the center of an international manhunt for her killer, John Patrick Addis.

Photo courtesy
Las Vegas Review-Journal

WANTED: MURDER/KIDNAP

JOHN PATRICK ADDIS

DOB 9/19/50
HT 6' 0" - 6' 1", WT 200,
Light Brown Hair
Blue-Green Eyes
AKA's JOHN H. EDWARDS,
DOB 5/11/50 AND
JOHN ELLIOT, (nfi)
Uses multiple Social
Security Numbers
FBI#115418HA7,
FPC:POPMQIPIPO/
18POPIP19,
NIC#W094641344

On August 19, 1995, Joann H. Albanese (remains found), disappeared from her residence in Las Vegas, NV, along with her boyfriend John Edwards. Investigation revealed Edwards true identity to be John Patrick Addis, an ex-police investigator, who was a certified instructor in crime scene and death investigations; a skilled marksman, survivalist and pilot; and found to be adept in manufacturing false identification. Our investigation has established a history of Addis meeting women at health clubs, where he would be a member or employee; aligning himself with a woman; moving in with her; and eventually leaving abruptly, often defrauding the woman of money. Our investigation has traced Addis through numerous states throughout the United States, however there has been no indication of additional women he has been associated with as missing or deceased. Our investigation has culminated in the issuance of a warrant for Addis' arrest for Kidnapping and Murder of Joann H. Albanese. Anyone with information regarding Addis' whereabouts are asked to contact the Las Vegas metropolitan Police Department, Federal Bureau of Investigation or your local police department.

Las Vegas Metropolitan Police Department
(702) 229-3111   ORI NV0020100   OCA 950820-1858

This poster was issued by Las Vegas police after Addis was indicted on murder and kidnapping charges in the disappearance of Joann Albanese.
Photo from Las Vegas police files

Laura Liliana Casillas Padilla is pictured in a missing persons photo distributed in Mexico after she vanished in the company of "John Charles Stone" in 1997.
Photo from Las Vegas police files

John Patrick Addis is pictured standing in a park in Guadalajara in a photo collected as evidence by investigators with the U.S. State Department and the Federal Bureau of Investigation.
Photo from Las Vegas police files

John Patrick Addis is pictured in a snapshot taken with his girlfriend, Laura Liliana Casillas Padilla, shortly before she disappeared from her Guadalajara home. The photo was collected by federal investigators and Las Vegas police and distributed in the search for Laura Liliana.
Photo from Las Vegas police files

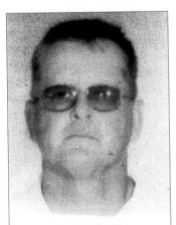

JHON CHARLES STONE
(A) J. CHARLES PETERSON
DOM. 4664 CAPE CORAL
PINE ISLAND 33915-00000
(A) JHON C. STONE
DOM. 4664 CAPE CORAL
PINE ISLAND 33915-00000

This is the last known photo ever taken of John Patrick Addis. Looking older and worn down, the Mexican identification card photo was taken under his Mexican alias, John Stone. He later adopted the alias J. Charles Peterson while in Chiapas, Mexico.
Photo from Las Vegas police files

Koch remained friends with both Tom and Joann Albanese after the divorce as well. Koch said it was roughly two years after the divorce, in 1995, when Joann called her and said she thought she finally had found a man who might work out. Joann told Koch she had a new boyfriend.

He was a beefy hunk named John Edwards.

"She called me and said, 'I met this very nice gentleman,' and, 'Oh, is he a hunk!'" Koch recalled. "She said, 'I saw him at the gym, at the health club,' or something like this, and 'we all have to go out next week together. I can tell you everything about it.'"

There were tentative plans for Joann to go out with the Kochs in a few weeks so Eli could meet this new boyfriend. Koch, however, had a family emergency with a relative to tend to in Brazil and was unable to go out to dinner with Joann and her new boyfriend.

She would never talk to Joann again.

13 ... THERE'S SOMETHING NOT
RIGHT WITH HIM

In 1995, Tara Rivera was a little self-conscious about her weight. She's a perfectly attractive and self-confident woman, but she said she still felt like she needed to shed a few pounds. As a result, she started searching for a gym to take care of what she, at least, viewed as a problem, and she settled on the World's Gym in Las Vegas at Tropicana Avenue and Eastern Boulevard. The facility is a typical workout factory: a single-story, warehouse-type commercial structure transformed into an expansive gymnasium complete with treadmills, weight machines, exercise classes, televisions, beat-pumping music, and personal-fitness instructors you can hire to help you get back in shape with a little sweat and discipline.

"I've always been little, petite sizes three to five, but as the years went by and I had kids, I gained a little weight, and [I was] struggling with it," she said. "So, I joined the gym, and for that, I got a free fitness instructor. I then hired one thereafter."

The fitness instructor assigned to Rivera was John Edwards. He was big, buff, handsome, incredibly friendly, and charming. Edwards, Rivera said, wasn't her type, but she did like him, and he seemed to be a quality individual.

"Personally, he was not my kind of guy," Rivera said. "My husband is Puerto Rican, and I like Latin men for some reason. I grew up in Queens, but if I'd grown up in an all-white neighborhood, then maybe."

"He had a very German, very chiseled look," Rivera recalled. "Blond hair, deep eyes, very chiseled at the jaw. He was very big and buff. A weightlifter, personal trainer, and very well taken care of."

Rivera trained at the gym three or four times with Edwards. Over time, Edwards told her he was single, didn't have any kids, and had never been married. Edwards was from Florida and rode a motorcycle. He talked little about his family, saying only that one of his parents was deceased, and that he didn't speak with the rest of his family. Slowly, Rivera started contemplating the idea of setting up her friend, Joann Albanese, on a date with Edwards. Joann, she knew, was on the hunt for a good man, and she figured Joann would like a man like Edwards.

"After the first initial visit to the gym, I went back three or four more times, and I approached him and said, 'You know, I've got this great girl. She's my best friend, she's divorced with two children, [and you guys should go out on a date].'

"I thought at the time that he was a great guy, a perfect guy for her," Rivera said. "He was forty-five, single, never been married, no children. She had so much going for her, and I thought they'd make a great couple [and] you would think the womanly instinct would say, 'Hey, something must be wrong with this guy,' but because he seemed like a sweetheart, and was such a real charmer, I figured I'd try it. Joann really needs to meet somebody nice.

"I told him all about her, and said, 'Would you be willing to go out on a date?'" Rivera recalled. "He said yes, so then I told Joann about him. She was like, 'Really? I'll go.'"

The couple went out on a dinner date a few days later. The following morning Joann called Rivera and blurted out, "I really like him!"

"Shortly after that, a couple of times afterward, we all went out and we all got together and it was clear they were very much involved," Rivera said. "I introduced them somewhere around March or April. Soon after, they started dating, and they just became very close. When they first started dating, he was wonderful to her. Everything was great."

Rivera thought at first that she'd done her friend Joann a huge favor. But within a couple of months, she would come to regret very deeply her decision to set Joann up with "John Edwards."

"Unfortunately, I introduced him to her," Rivera said.

Kevin Hemerick Cyrus was, in 1995, a general manager for World's Gym on Tropicana Avenue in Las Vegas. He met John Edwards in late 1994 when Edwards showed up at the gym and asked for a tour of the facility.

"I was at the gym working the counter," Cyrus said. "He came in asking to take a tour of the gym, and me, thinking that he wanted to be a member, gave him a full tour, [and] as we wrapped up the tour, he started telling me that he had worked in the fitness industry and that he was looking for a job. He told me he'd [been to college] and majored in kinesiology. He was a tennis instructor, ski instructor, and a few other things. I told him I'd have to talk to him at a later date and then I realized the owner was there. I made an introduction to the owner, and the next day we hired him."

Edwards filled out a W-4 tax form and provided a résumé saying he'd been the owner of multiple fitness businesses in Cape Coral, Florida. He also produced a Florida driver's license. He worked as a fitness instructor at both this gym and another gym in Las Vegas, 24-Hour Fitness, for the next four to six months. He earned a meager $4.25 an hour but also received commissions for his personal-fitness training and was given some minor financial incentives for signing up new members.

Edwards, it seemed to his colleagues, was a very intelligent man. He knew a lot about physical fitness, and he was an avid weight lifter.

"He was also a writer, and he had written a screenplay for a movie that was going to be made," Cyrus said. "I [was given] the opportunity to look at it, but I never did. He passed it around to a few people."

Cyrus last saw Edwards in the summer of 1995 when he showed up at the gym and announced he was headed to California to help with the movie to be made from his alien-abductions screenplay.

"He asked for a leave of absence, stating the screenplay he had written finally got accepted, they were going to turn that into a movie, and he had to go to Hollywood to collaborate with whoever was putting it together," Cyrus said.

_____

Glenn R. Wilcox Jr., forty-eight, is a real estate broker who met Edwards in 1995 at another Las Vegas gym, 24-Hour Fitness, in northwest Las Vegas. Wilcox had recently lost fifty pounds working out and getting into shape. At the time, he was looking to get out of the Las Vegas hotel-gaming business, and with his new physique he picked up a transitional job as a fitness instructor. He worked with Edwards at 24-Hour Fitness, and he came to like the man. Edwards told him he used to be a cop in Alaska, that he loved to hunt, and he talked a lot about living out in the woods and being able to survive in remote areas with very little.

Edwards told Wilcox he was just divorced and starting over. Wilcox observed that Edwards was highly disciplined when it came to his health, and he was impressed with Edwards's fitness regimen.

"He was Mr. Nutrition," Wilcox said. "He was a real good mountain-man type. I knew he was a real outdoorsman. I just pictured all that from being in Alaska with all his camping gear and stuff. He lifted a lot, and he would help us train. He played tennis a lot. . . . A really fit kind of a guy. Sandy blondish brown hair, short [and] well-trimmed, and what I remember about him is sometimes his eyes took on a different look when he got serious about something. They got real strong when he got serious.

"I got the impression that he was very intelligent," Wilcox said. "He knew a lot about fitness and nutrition. Everyone in top management would come to him with questions. They'd tell him their whole story, and he had an answer on what they ought to do. Everyone looked up to him. Regarding fitness and nutrition, he knew that stuff inside out."

Wilcox eventually agreed to let Edwards rent a room in the home he was renting in the northwest section of the Las Vegas Valley. When Edwards moved in, Wilcox noticed Edwards didn't really have much in the way of belongings at all. He didn't even have a bed.

"He was sleeping on a sleeping bag, and he mostly had a bunch of camping stuff," Wilcox said. "I saw he had a box full of *Penthouse* magazines."

He also noticed Edwards had a dark blue pickup, and he acted a little strangely in the way he parked the vehicle in front of the home.

"He used to back his truck up in my yard, to the side of the house, all the way up against the brick wall," Wilcox said, adding he would later suspect Addis was trying to hide his license plate.

Edwards opened up to him a little bit in the two weeks they lived together, revealing that he'd once been a cop and been in a dispute with his prior wife. Edwards implied that he'd gotten into a little bit of trouble over him keeping custody of his kids longer than he was supposed to.

"He briefly told me a story that his wife was taking the kids, so he took the kids and took off, and he ended up getting caught," Wilcox said. "He implied there were some ramifications. I knew there was trouble over it. I was assuming that was why he wasn't on the force anymore."

Edwards seemed to be a very well-traveled man. He talked about Alaska and Michigan and even indicated he'd traveled abroad. He spoke frequently of Mexico and his fondness for it. Wilcox also talked about his own personal faith with Edwards. Wilcox volunteered that he was a Christian, and Edwards told him he'd completely rejected the contents of the Bible. Edwards's face changed, Wilcox said, and he took on a very serious look when the two men talked about this topic.

"You could see it in his eyes," Wilcox said. "I believe in the Bible, and John said, 'Those are just stories!' He was very adamant the Bible is all wrong. That's one time I saw [a physical change in his facial expression and eyes]. He was very adamant that the Bible was just a bunch of stories with no truth to it."

Wilcox came to learn his roommate was dating a woman named Joann, and one thing that stands out in his memory about the relationship was that the two argued a lot. In one instance, Edwards was on the phone with Joann at 24-Hour Fitness, and Wilcox could hear Joann yelling at Edwards over the phone even though he was sitting across the room.

"They fought a lot, and at some point I got the idea she wanted him to do more than work at 24-Hour Fitness," Wilcox said. "[She felt] that he could do so much more. John was pretty much a genius, and he wasn't doing anything with it. So they would have screaming matches, and one time [at the gym] she was yelling at him so loud you could hear her across the room over the phone. . . . He got up, set the phone down, walked around, would come back, and she [hadn't stopped screaming]. He was like, 'Yeah, uh huh,' and she never even took a breath the whole time. He laughed about it."

Despite the tensions between the two, they apparently got along at times because Edwards at one point wanted Wilcox to go on a vacation with him and Joann to Mexico.

"He was trying to hook me up with one of Joann's girlfriends, and, together, we could all go down to Mexico for a few days or a week," Wilcox said. "I knew he liked Mexico."

Joann Albanese's sister in Las Vegas, Dollie Greenrock Wells, is a Realtor who was very close to her sister. She first met Joann's new boyfriend, "John Edwards," in approximately April of 1995 at Pistol Pete's restaurant in Las Vegas. Edwards and Joann showed up at a birthday party for a child who was related to Wells. Wells would later tell authorities she didn't like Edwards from the moment she met him. She just had a strange feeling about him. She thought it was strange that this buff man, who many women would find very attractive, was chasing after her sister—a divorced single mom with two kids. She suspected Edwards saw a mark in her sister because she had a very nice home in The Lakes, and Edwards apparently had nothing.

"I didn't like him," Wells would later tell Las Vegas authorities. "I didn't want to talk with him. I walked away."

The relationship between Joann and Edwards evolved very rapidly, by all accounts. Within a few months, Edwards was staying several nights a week at Joann's house in The Lakes. Her daughters would tell authorities they were apprehensive about this new man who they knew only as "John," and shortly after Edwards started showing up at the house they noticed some spats between their mother and the new man.

"I would describe their relationship as sometimes fine, sometimes not," Amber Albanese would later say. "They would sometimes scream and argue."

Eventually, though, Amber Albanese would become very uncomfortable when John Edwards was around. For some reason, he made her uneasy.

"There was a fight [and] I had my mom throw him out," Amber Albanese said. "I didn't trust him in the house."

Tara Rivera found John Edwards, at first, to be very likable and loving to Joann. This changed, however, roughly a month after the two started dating. Tara and Joann were very close friends. They worked together at the MGM Grand, and on their days off they talked to each other on the phone regularly. Sometimes they talked on the phone at least twice a day. She was perhaps the person closest to Joann outside of her immediate family. Rivera said she was surprised to learn that, within a month, Edwards was staying at Joann's house in The Lakes. It seemed a little quick for Edwards to be moving in. It was always Joann who was paying for everything when the couple went out. Joann paid for Edwards's meals, for gas in his truck, and yet they always used Joann's Toyota—not Edwards's pickup.

"He like worshipped the ground she walked on, but then it went way above and beyond what would be normal as the relationship progressed," Rivera said.

Rivera and her husband went to dinner a few times with the couple, and she started to feel like Edwards was acting "obsessive" toward Joann. She described his demeanor toward Joann as controlling.

"It seemed weird that she never went to his house," Rivera said. "It was never in his vehicle. It was always her vehicle, her house, and it was like he was weaseling his way into her home and sleeping over every day and it was like he lived there. He also had very few belongings, and I found that strange. He could pack his entire life up in a box. It started to get a little bit controlling."

"Just not the lifestyle she's used to," Rivera said. "The lifestyle she's used to is someone that caters to her and spends on her, [and] not [one] that she pays and does everything in the relationship."

There were some conversations between Rivera and Joann that indicated to Rivera that Joann was considering dumping Edwards. Around this time, she said, Edwards unexpectedly showed up at her front door. He was sweating and had ridden his bicycle a very long way—all the way across the entire city of Las Vegas—to visit Rivera and her husband. He said he was there to talk because he was worried Joann was going to cut him loose.

"He came to the house by bicycle, all the way from his home, and we were a little taken aback because we were not buddy-buddy," Rivera said. "[He said] he loved me to death. He owed me the world for introducing him to Joann, and that anything I ever wanted or needed . . . I could always come to him. He could never repay me enough.

"So he's sitting there, crying, saying, 'Please help me! I don't want to lose her!' " Rivera recalled. "He was weeping and pitiful."

Rivera thought the incident was strange, but what happened next caused major alarms to go off. On May 3, 1995, she and her husband went out to dinner with Joann and Edwards, and during a routine conversation, she said she saw Edwards change physically right in front of her eyes. Rivera was just casually conversing and mentioned that she was still struggling with losing a few pounds. She didn't think anything about the comment as she joked to Edwards, her personal trainer, "John you've got to help me!"

Without prompting, Edwards completely flipped out over the seemingly innocuous comment.

"I said, 'John, you've got to help me! I'm always bitching about my weight!' " Rivera said. He turned around, angrily yelling, and said, according to Rivera, " 'I told you! I'm the best! I owe you my life.' "

Edwards said he owed Rivera his life for introducing him to Joann, but Rivera found the incident to be completely chilling.

"He flipped out and started pounding the table, and he got really weird," Rivera said.

"And he got louder, and people were looking and staring, and I got very uncomfortable at that time," she said. "He was saying, 'When are you going to realize I'll do anything for you!' "

Beyond the completely inappropriate response to the innocuous comment, Rivera saw an expression on Edwards's face that frightened her. His eyes seemed to swell outward from his face. The veins in his temples were engorged, and she would later describe the look as demented.

"He just snapped," Rivera said. "Jekyll and Hyde. I observed an outrage, like his eyes were bulging. Deranged."

"At that point, I squeezed my husband's leg and said, 'It's time to go. Now,' " Rivera said.

That night, Rivera told her husband she was going to warn Joann the next day that she should seriously consider getting rid of Edwards.

"I said to my husband, 'He's off. There's something wrong with him,' " Rivera recalled. "There is something not right about him."

The next day she called Joann and told her to dump her new boyfriend because he frightened her.

"I said, 'There's something I've got to tell you,' " Rivera recalled. " 'I've got this eerie feeling.' I said, 'I think you need to get rid of him. There's something wrong.' "

Joann agreed and revealed to Rivera some personal

details about the couple's relationship that frightened Rivera even more. She said Edwards was implementing near complete control over her life. He wanted her to walk around the house all day long, naked, and he required Joann to have sex with him multiple times a day to the point where Joann was in pain because of the nonstop sex. Joann also told Rivera she was not allowed to go to the bathroom without Edwards being present.

"He would want her to stay naked all day and he would sleep with her all day," Rivera said. "It would hurt her."

Edwards insisted, after sex, that he stay on top of Joann and stay inside of her while they slept.

"She wasn't allowed to put her clothes on," Rivera said. "He used to sleep with his penis inside her. She was afraid of him."

"He's *sooooo* controlling!" Joann told her friend. "I can't pee without him standing there in the doorway watching."

"I can't even breathe," Joann said, crying. "I can't take this anymore!"

Both women were concerned about having Edwards near Joann's daughters.

"I said, 'When he's in the shower, you need to go through his wallet, check his I.D., and do a background check on him,'" Rivera said. "'It's gone too fast. He's weaseled his way into your life. He's using your credit cards, your money, you are always paying. He's on a motorcycle. He has this truck, yet you've never been to his apartment?' I didn't have a good feeling."

Rivera assumed Joann was going to dump Edwards for good, but she was shocked when, the next time she talked to Joann, "She's telling me they are planning a trip to Hawaii and, lo and behold, he came up with half the money."

The couple returned from Hawaii, and Joann told Rivera the couple had a "good time" but that Edwards was "completely controlling" during the entire trip.

"She felt smothered," Rivera said. "She said, 'I can't get my nails done [and] I can't do anything without him.' They had a good time but he was completely overbearing. She couldn't even walk on the beach alone. He never explained himself ever. That [was] just his personality. She felt that she was ready to end the relationship."

Around the same time, Joann and Edwards met with Joann's mother. Edwards blurted out to Joann's mother, Margarete Greenrock, that he wanted to marry her daughter.

"He wanted to marry her," Greenrock would later tell Las Vegas authorities. "[He wanted to know] if I could help him to marry her."

Greenrock told Edwards that Joann wasn't ready: "I don't pick my children's husbands. It's between them, you know."

Joann was listening to the conversation and interjected.

"He says to me, 'Would you please help me and tell Joann that she [should] marry me?'" Greenrock said. "And she turned around, and she said, 'John, I told you, when I'm ready, I'll let you know. Don't bother my mom with this.'"

On August 18, 1995, Joann called Rivera and said it was official: she was definitely kicking Edwards to the curb, and she had a plan for how to do it. She was going to take him out to dinner at a fancy restaurant at the Las Vegas Hilton and tell him it was over, that she just couldn't do it anymore, and that she was unhappy. She hoped he would understand.

"I never heard from her again," Rivera said.

14 ... VANISHED

Dollie Greenrock Wells had a very creepy encounter with her sister's boyfriend, John Edwards, in early August 1995. She was meeting a friend, her sister, Joann, and Edwards at Joann's house, and then the four were planning to go out to dinner at a Las Vegas restaurant called the Dive. Wells already knew she didn't like Edwards. She thought there was something wrong with him, and she just didn't like the feeling he gave her. Her sister always paid for Edwards's food and drinks. The couple, when traveling, always drove her car, and there were concerns that Edwards might be abusing Joann. What happened that night, though, at the Dive only further escalated Wells's concerns about her sister's new boyfriend.

Over dinner and drinks, Edwards was talking about Arizona and a rather desolate location called Little Hell Canyon, near Prescott. Edwards talked about its remoteness, and Wells wasn't impressed with the description Edwards gave.

"I said, 'It sounds like an awful place,'" Wells recalled. "He said, 'Actually, it's a really beautiful place,' and he thought that he might be going there soon."

Then the conversation between Wells and Edwards turned to hunting. Wells liked to hunt small game. She was good with a firearm. Edwards spoke about how he'd hunted big game.

"My sister had brought up the fact that I liked to hunt," Wells said. "He had asked me what was the largest game I'd ever hunted. I said, 'Small things like quail, deer,' you know, things like that. And he said he didn't mean small in size. He meant small in intelligence.

"And I looked at him, and I just said . . . that a human was the only thing intelligent and no, I've never hunted human. He looked at me and said, 'I would.'"

The comment gave Wells chills. As the evening played out, Edwards seemed to be very uncomfortable. He wanted to leave, but Joann didn't.

"He became more angry with her and frustrated with her," Wells said. "He wanted to leave and she wanted to stay."

Wells avoided talking to Edwards the rest of the night.

August 18, 1995, was a scorching-hot Friday in Las Vegas. It was also the day that Joann Albanese and her ex-husband, Tom, were scheduled to exchange the children for the weekend. She was planning to go out to dinner that night with her new boyfriend of five months, John Edwards. Friends said she was going to terminate the relationship with her controlling, obsessive boyfriend. Joann Albanese talked to her daughters early that morning before they left for the weekend with their dad.

"I saw her at 7 a.m., and it was the last time I saw my mother," Amber Albanese said.

According to Las Vegas police reports, Joann Albanese was at work on Saturday, August 19, and was last seen by her supervisor leaving the office for the day. At 6 p.m. that Saturday she talked to her mother, Margarete Greenrock, and said she was going out to dinner with Edwards and was going to end the relationship.

"[I talked to her] on the phone for a good twenty-five minutes," Greenrock would later tell authorities. "She told me, 'Mom, I cleaned the whole house. I got one more bathroom to do, and I got to take a shower. John's coming later on.'

"They made a reservation for dinner in the Hilton, and [she told me], 'I want to tell him that I'm not ready to be married.' I said, 'Be careful. You've got to know what you're doing.' "

On August 19, 1995, Glenn Wilcox was already scheduled to work a full day at the 24-Hour Fitness gym where John Edwards worked. That day, Edwards showed up and asked Wilcox if he could cover his shift that night. Edwards said he was going out to a very fancy restaurant with his girlfriend, Joann. Wilcox accepted the offer. He needed the money and was willing to cover for his roommate.

"He and Joann were going to some kind of function, and I believe he had to rent a tuxedo," Wilcox said. "I covered the shift. I worked a day, then had to cover his night shift."

The weekend went off without incident for Joann's children. Around noon on Saturday, Amber decided to call her mom. She called her at home and got no answer. The following day, a Sunday, August 20, Tom Albanese drove the children back to The Lakes. He watched as Amber, followed closely by Brittany, used her garage door opener to open the garage door, and the children walked in the house.

"Approximately 6 p.m. on Sunday evening," Tom Albanese would say. "Amber had the garage door opener, so she opened up the garage door and Joann's car wasn't in there, but I did notice her boyfriend's truck at the top of the cul-de-sac. I just knew him as John. I only saw him one time, and I didn't really ever talk to him.

"I told the girls to go in and get cleaned up. Wait for their mom. If she was ever going to be gone, she would call if she was going to be late," Tom Albanese said. "She would say, 'Tom, I'll pick up the girls at your house.' So I didn't notice anything unusual when I dropped off the girls. I told them to get cleaned up. I went back to my house. I was exhausted from the day's activities, and I had fallen asleep."

Amber Albanese would later recall for a Las Vegas grand jury that she sensed something was wrong almost immediately after entering the home.

"My sister and I went into the house, and I noticed that all the lights were on," she recalled. "And, that's very rare [because my mom's] a person that's set in her ways. The lights are never—all those lights are never on. I said, 'Mom, where are you?'"

"She wasn't there," Amber said. "I went over, and I noticed that the door that led into the house was unlocked. Her car was gone. Then I said, 'Oh my gosh. What happened?'"

Panic swept through the teen like a cold wind. She and her sister were home alone in the house, their mother wasn't there, and Amber knew something wasn't right.

Brittany seemed to sense something was wrong as well. The younger girl started to cry, and Amber tried to console her little sister, telling her everything was going to be okay. In the coming hours, Amber would be questioned about whether it was really unusual that her mother wasn't home, but Amber knew. It was unusual for her mom to go somewhere without telling them. Her mom was just always there. Joann was a creature of habit—someone who made meticulous lists and who kept a rigid, by-the-book schedule for everything. She was always on time, and if she wasn't, she called.

"Very consistent on everything that she does," Amber said. "Everything. She'd write out a list for the nanny or whoever was taking care of us for them to follow the list, numbers of where she's going to be, what time to do this, what time to do that. You know, basically all the rules that go on.

"She is always home when my sister and I get home," Amber said. "She got us to go bathe and put us to bed, or whatever. Then I went upstairs, and her door was open, and that is never unlocked and rarely opened.

"Her jewelry's in there," Amber said of the bedroom. "Her money's in there. She's got birth certificates for my sister and I, her birth certificate. Just a lot of personal belongings that shouldn't be tampered with when she's gone. Me and my sister had a nanny that took care of us, and that door was always locked."

The bedroom door had a bolt lock with a key. Amber said when Joann wasn't home, she always locked the door.

"The door, it's never opened. . . . [But it] was wide open," Amber said. "Even when my parents were together, it was always [closed] and locked."

Amber walked through the bedroom and noticed some

other odd occurrences that troubled her greatly. It seemed to Amber that some of her mom's belongings were slightly out of place. It didn't look as if the room had been rummaged through or ransacked, but items seemed to be slightly askew, and two pillows and a blanket that were usually on the bed were gone. In the bathroom on a sink counter, there was some brown packing tape. It was a thick type of tape Amber had never seen before.

"That was never in our home, ever," Amber said. "We have a clear tape that's exactly the same, but it's clear, not brown."

Amber then noticed two facts that sealed in her mind the belief that something was terribly wrong. When looking through her mother's dresser, Amber noticed her mother's purse, with her wallet and identification cards, in a drawer. Next to the purse were Joann's watch and bracelet. Her mother never, ever left the home without her purse, and she never, ever just left her jewelry in the dresser. She always wore her jewelry, except when she was in the shower.

"It was very unusual that her belongings were there because she takes her purse with her," Amber said. "It's got her money, her driver's license, everything. I believe her keys were even there. One of her sets of keys."

"Even if she's going across the street, she brings [her purse] with her," Amber said. "[And] I did notice her jewelry. She had her watch that never gets taken off unless she goes and takes a shower, and her bracelet. The purse, the door open, the tape, the pillows off the bed, was enough to know that there was something going on because [it] was very strange. This is not a normal routine that goes on in the home."

Amber wondered whether her mother's new boyfriend, John, could be responsible for her mother's absence. She

knew the blond-haired man only as John, and she knew
very little about the man even though he'd stayed at Joann's
home, on and off, for several weeks. Amber knew he was
a personal trainer, and that he drove an old 1980s-era Ford
Ranger pickup, but she didn't even know the man's last
name. She was very uncomfortable in his presence. The
relationship between John and her mother had been going
on for only a few months, Amber said, and it was somewhat stormy. Amber would later recall she was uneasy
around her mother's new boyfriend.

Amber, convinced that something was seriously wrong,
called two people: her father and her nanny, Diane Smith.
She told them all of the suspicious details and how her
mother's gold Honda Accord was gone and that John's
truck was parked about fifty yards down the street. Both
Smith and Tom Albanese tried to calm Amber down,
thinking there must be some innocent explanation for
Joann's whereabouts. Tom Albanese urged his daughter to
take a deep breath, wait a few hours, and call him back.
He was sure Joann was probably out running an errand
and had simply lost track of time. He was sure she'd walk
through the front door any minute.

"I got a call from Amber. Amber said, 'Mom's . . . not
home,'" Tom Albanese recalled. "The tone in her voice
was worried, and I told her just to hang in there and hung
up. I went back to sleep."

Amber knew something was wrong even though her
dad didn't think the matter was serious. She decided to call
the police after her father hung up the phone, and when
she relayed the details of her mother's missing status to the
dispatcher, the response she got infuriated her even more.

"I called the police, and they said, 'Well, we can't do

anything because it hasn't been twenty-four hours,' "
Amber said. "So I flipped out on them on the phone."

The dispatcher was alarmed and sent a female officer to
the house. In the meantime, Amber called her father again,
and this time, he, too, was alarmed. It had been hours and
his ex-wife was nowhere to be found.

"A couple hours later, I got a call from Amber, 'Mom's
still not there, and I called the police,' " Tom Albanese
said. "And, all of a sudden, the lady officer was on the
phone to me."

Around the same time, Joann's sister, Dollie Greenrock
Wells, called over to her sister's home because her mother,
Margarete, had not heard from Joann in two days. Wells
was startled when a Las Vegas police officer answered the
phone. She confirmed that Joann had not come home. Like
everyone else, Wells knew something wasn't right, and she
worried John Edwards was responsible. The female officer
took Amber and Brittany and drove them to their father's
house. A sense of shock overcame Tom Albanese when the
officer showed up at his home with his daughters.

Joann, he knew, would never leave the children home
alone for this long without calling.

"The lady officer had dropped off Amber and Brittany
back over to my house, and this was probably around 11,
11:30 on Sunday night," Tom Albanese said.

Everyone in the family sensed something was very
wrong. They didn't hear anything from Joann all night,
and there was no way she would ever go an entire night
without at least calling.

"I took care of the children from that point forward and
in hopes that I would hear from their mother," Tom Albanese said.

The next day Tom Albanese went to his ex-wife's home.

"Her bed wasn't made and stuff was all on the floor," Tom Albanese said. "That was unusual because Joann was a fairly tidy person. The door was open. The master bedroom was open. It was unusual because when I was married to her we had put a lock on it as you would on the outside of the house," Tom Albanese said.

"We had problems with sitters going in our bedroom and taking things, and to alleviate that, we always locked the door, even if we went to the grocery store. [Seeing the bedroom door open was] highly unusual. That wouldn't happen. She always locked it."

Next to a phone in the kitchen Tom Albanese noticed a receipt from JCPenney for a 50 percent payment Joann had made on some window coverings. There was a date on the receipt indicating the window coverings were to be installed the first part of September, and this would later be considered evidence by authorities that Joann had no intentions of just taking off with John Addis and leaving everything behind. The condition of the bedroom, though, was what confirmed for Tom Albanese that something very suspicious was going on. He knew the habits of his wife very well. She was meticulous about every detail. The bed was always made immediately, and her personal belongings were never left lying around.

"[The bed] was not made, and I noticed that the comforter was off to the side," Tom Albanese said. "Very unusual. Joann would always make up the bed before she left for the day unless she was in a rush to get out of there. That was very unusual to see the bed in that condition.

"Plus, also, I noticed that her hair dryer and curling iron were on the vanity," he said. "She would normally put those away in the drawer. Her purse was there, which was very unusual with her wallet and her other belongings, and then there [were] some clothes scattered [all] over."

Tom Albanese said Joann would always take her pillows with her whenever she traveled.

"Always, always," he said, adding that "she would always bring her bed pillow in her suitcase because she despised pillows in hotels."

On Sunday, August 20, 1995, Dollie Greenrock Wells called over to her sister's house. Her mother, Margarete, was very worried because she hadn't heard from her daughter Joann.

"A police officer [answered the phone]," Wells would recall for a grand jury. "A female police officer."

Wells knew something was terribly wrong. Her sister would never leave the children alone. She heard nothing from her sister all night. Panicked, she started a frantic search the next morning.

"Very early that morning, I started calling the highway patrol and hospitals in all of the surrounding states to see if maybe there had been a flat tire or an accident or something like that reported," Wells recalled.

A number of important items were found in Joann Albanese's wallet, including credit cards, bank cards, and insurance information. Joann would not leave her credit cards and money behind and just leave the house like that.

"There was less than fifty dollars [in the purse], and through that purse and other purses, there was loose change," Wells said, adding she found her sister's passport in her sister's bedroom. Her sister's watch and bracelet were also in the dresser drawer, next to the purse. Wells did a full search, "opening drawers to find things in the bedroom."

"My mother requested that her jewelry be removed in case . . . [Edwards] came back to get it," Wells said. "Her watch and her bracelet.

"Then we started putting out fliers," Wells said. "I personally walked around the downtown area for many hours and days distributing fliers to various places—bars, restaurants, places of business, everywhere, dry cleaners, haircutting places. I would even go down there late at night and hand out flyers in biker bars and places like that. Any place that I thought he might be able to be found."

From the time of Wells's creepy encounter with Edwards, she never saw her sister again. There was no way Joann would have just walked away from her daughters, the center of her life, not to mention her life in Las Vegas, which she thoroughly enjoyed, complete with a valuable home and bank assets and the chance to continue to travel the world. She also left a paycheck and a half she never collected.

Wells never heard a word from her beloved sister again. It was as if she'd vanished off the face of the earth.

15 . . . HANNA

Larry Hanna certainly knows what it means to sacrifice for the purposes of the public good. He watched his father, Bud, survive through decades of pain and physical suffering, and the man never complained a day. Bud Hanna was cut practically in half by machine-gun fire while helping make the Allied push in Normandy. He was literally left to die but made a full recovery and came back to the United States to provide for his family while working as a plumber in St. Louis.

"He's been living on borrowed time since June 16, 1944," Hanna said. "He . . . got cut in half by machine-gun fire in Normandy. He was hit at least three times, bullets out his back. They triaged him, and at that point it was, 'How bad is he?' They thought there was no way he would live, so the medics shot him full of morphine and put him in a corner to die. Later on, when they went back, he was still living, so they managed to piece him back together."

"The surgeons had to rebuild his entire system, take out most of his stomach, rebuild his intestines," Hanna said. "The military put him back together, he went to school for plumbing and heating and air conditioning, and he supported our family and never complained once."

The sacrifice his father made in World War II is something very special to Hanna. Watching the movie *Band of Brothers*, which documented the profound sacrifices of World War II vets in combat, is something that Hanna found particularly moving. He watched what happened after his dad came home from battle and the courage the man demonstrated as a husband and father for decades.

"The *Band of Brothers* movie and the book *The Greatest Generation*, also about World War II—it really rings home for me," Hanna said. "He never talked too much about the war, and it wasn't until the movie *Saving Private Ryan* came out that I got a real serious interest in what he went through.

"Once he started talking about it, it made me realize that most people couldn't live through that and not be half goofy," Hanna said. "He's from a different era. An amazing man."

Hanna relies on the life lessons of endurance and strength taught to him by his father as he works his way through the underbelly of Las Vegas as a homicide detective for the Las Vegas Metropolitan Police Department. Hanna is, by all standards, an old-school cop. He's got wavy blondish gray hair and a moustache, and he's the type of guy who can look you over and, you just know, by looking at him, that he's already got you pegged in his mind. He's been a witness to human behavior, criminality, and justice as a Las Vegas cop for nearly three decades now, so he knows what humans are like. He knows how they act and how they think. He's very good at what he does, which is catching the Las Vegas Valley's most dangerous killers and criminals. He's thorough and tough, and he has little acceptance for games from criminal offenders. He's a man who has given his life to law enforcement because he believes it's the right thing to do. He works on behalf of the public. He works hard, and oftentimes, he thinks about the example his father gave him when times are difficult— when cases are cold, when information is scarce, or when witnesses are reluctant.

"What did I learn from my father?" Hanna says. "A great work ethic. You don't quit. You keep going, and be happy with what you've got."

Born in Memphis, Tennessee, in the 1950s, Larry Hanna grew up in a loving family with two brothers. Bud and his wife, Mary, were exemplary parents, and Mary worked as a secretary in the St. Louis school district to help make ends meet. Hanna himself served in the military and briefly thought about a career as a writer or a journalist.

"Either a DJ or a writer," Hanna said of his early ambitions in life. "I watched all the Jack Webb police shows, and then I met a St. Louis copper who lived in an apartment complex I lived in, and he got me on to the St. Louis Police Department."

"Being a cop is kind of like being a reporter," Hanna said. "You want to find out what's going on. Well, inside the yellow tape, though, it's much more interesting. I'll also say that when I first joined the St. Louis Police Department, I was a flaming liberal. A few short years on the streets of St. Louis, and I lost that real quick."

In addition to being a good cop, Hanna is also quite the

colorful character and a straight shooter who doesn't hesitate to tell you how policing has changed over the last two
decades.

"Everything is different," Hanna said. "When I was a
young buck, running around, being a cop, when you got
off work, you went out and got hammered. You and your
squad would go out somewhere and get absolutely plowed.
Young guys now, they go to the police substation and
play Xbox. What the fuck? You are playing video games?
There's alcohol and women out there. Come on. Back then
it was alcohol, women, and police work."

Hanna came to Las Vegas for a better opportunity in
1981. The benefits for cops in Vegas were better. "So I
came out here and never looked back."

"It's changed," Hanna said. "The laws are different. The
people are different. It's a lot more structured, and it's not
as much fun. Physically and mentally, trying to work patrol
right now, I'd be in too much trouble. You give me a Taser
out on the street, it'd be like American Bandstand! If we'd
had those back then, oh God."

He worked in patrol for sixteen years and left the Las
Vegas police to work for the Federal Air Marshal Service
for about a year and half. He returned to the Las Vegas
police force in 1989, worked juvenile investigations, then
made it into the Missing Persons Detail. He has solved literally hundreds of violent crimes, murders, and disappear-
ances, but like any good cop, he thinks a lot about the cases
in which he wasn't able to bring the perpetrator to justice.
Two cases stand out in this regard.

The first is the disappearance and likely murder of
Randy Evers in Las Vegas. The three-year-old was last seen
in his apartment in 1993. The boy's father fell asleep, and

when he woke, the child was gone. Randy Evers has never been found, and no one knows what happened to him.

"We had several persons of interest over the years, but the body was never found," Hanna said. "There was no evidence. It's a case that could make a career, break a career, or last a career, and I've had Randy since day one, and all the other investigators have since gone. I still stay in touch with the National Center for Missing and Exploited Children. Questions come in every once in a while about the case."

There is one other case in Hanna's long and distinguished career that frustrates Hanna to this day. It is the case of John Patrick Addis, and he is a man Hanna refers to as a ghost.

Hanna was working the Missing Persons Detail in 1995 when he first heard of Joann Albanese. The Missing Persons Detail had collected a missing-persons report on Joann from her loved ones. They were highly suspicious that she'd been kidnapped or the victim of foul play at the hands of her new boyfriend, John Edwards. Hanna didn't think much of the case when he first heard about it. A lot of boyfriends and girlfriends run off in Vegas and show up a few days or weeks later. Edwards, he was told, was a trainer at a local gym. The couple had been dating for roughly five months. The last anyone heard from Joann was on Saturday, August 19. That night, Edwards had showed up at a local gym and asked his friend, Glenn Wilcox, to cover his shift because he was going out to a function with Joann. Now Joann's gold Honda was missing.

"They'd had the report, and Todd Rosenberg, a detective

I worked with, went out to make contact with the family, just to do a cursory check," Hanna said. "On the surface, it didn't look like anything. I didn't think we would be on it. An adult woman and adult male didn't come home when they were supposed to. That happens in Las Vegas. People get sidetracked. They go their separate ways. So the report is taken and she's listed in the computer as missing. There's really nothing here for us to go on and get crazy about.

"So Todd went out there and did a cursory check of the residence and that was pretty much it," Hanna said. "Then the family called and said, 'You know, this guy's truck is out there,' " Hanna recalled. "I thought maybe they'd left in her car because her car's not here."

"So the [family] asked, 'Can we go look in his truck?' " Hanna recalled. "I told them, 'I don't care. If you find something to follow up on, give me a call.' "

Joann Albanese's sister, Dollie Greenrock Wells, was by now conducting a frantic search for her sister. Wells had never liked Edwards and had been concerned about his relationship with her sister. She gathered some family friends and, with Hanna's approval, set about to search Edwards's blue pickup on August 21.

"Larry Hanna asked us . . . to find anything like checking accounts, credit cards, anything that could help him show some kind of contact," Wells would tell a grand jury.

"My niece and I originally went there to find what Larry had requested," Wells said. "The second day, the Tuesday, the day before I met with Larry, is when we went there, my niece, my stepdad, and myself, to look in his truck."

Wells, with the help of her stepfather, was able to get into Edwards's pickup truck through a rear sliding window.

"We only did what he told us to do," Wells said. "To

find whatever we could that might help him. My stepdad opened the little rear widow. Camper windows or whatever, if you have a camper shell."

Inside the truck, Wells found a "résumé, some books, pictures, news articles, license plates from Washington. Actually there were two license plates. I don't recall where the other one was from. Various things like that."

What Wells found next in the vehicle caused the investigation into Joann's disappearance to shift into high gear. There were some IDs in the car with other men's names on them, and the tags were from Washington and Florida. There was an envelope with the printed words "John Addis" on it.

The multiple plates, names, and a different name on the envelope led the family to believe John Edwards wasn't who he said he was. Hanna ran the tag number on the plate and it was "dead," not registered to anyone. This was suspicious. On the night of August 22, John Edwards's truck was towed to the Las Vegas police tow-impound yard for safekeeping. Hanna, meanwhile, did some more digging on the stuff Wells had found in the pickup.

"There was a title in the vehicle that came out of Florida," Hanna said. "And when we contacted the last known owners of that vehicle, they said they had sold it in 1993 to an unknown person, and the title had never been changed over to anyone else's name.

"There was a Washington license plate that was basically dead," Hanna said. "It had no registration record at all. And some of the other information contained the name of a John Addis that had been printed on an envelope, and based on the information that we had gotten the previous day from where Mr. Edwards had used to work, we had obtained a Xerox copy of a Florida driver's license."

No one in the Albanese family had ever heard the name John Addis before. It was unclear whether or not this was another name for John Edwards.

"A different name and the plate didn't go to any vehicle," Hanna said. "And it was like, this ain't right. Things just weren't matching up. Whoever is driving this truck is concealing their identity. They aren't who they say they are."

The detectives went to Edwards's place of work at 24-Hour Fitness and obtained a copy of the driver's license Edwards had submitted when he applied for his job. Hanna saw Edwards's face for the first time, and he seemed like a clean-cut guy. The address Edwards listed on his license was in Cape Coral, Florida. Hanna called the Cape Coral Police Department and asked if they could go to the address listed on the license to see if anyone there might know anything about Edwards's whereabouts. Hanna was surprised when the Cape Coral police called back to say that John Edwards was actually at the house, but he was a six-feet-five Samoan with long black hair.

"They did, in fact, contact John Edwards, and he was a person who was substantially different than the John Edwards known in Las Vegas," Hanna said. "This gentleman was much larger and hadn't been to Las Vegas in over fifteen years. Basically his identification was stolen.

"What we began learning on the 22nd is that we weren't sure who we were dealing with, and that we may have a problem," Hanna said. "We placed [Joann's] name and her vehicle into the NCIC [the National Crime Information Center] . . . as an endangered missing person."

The next morning, Hanna, fellow detective Ray Brotherson, and Las Vegas police senior crime scene analyst David Ruffino went to Joann's home in The Lakes and

met with most of Joann's family. Dollie Greenrock Wells
was there, as was Jack Williams, an associate of Joann's
mother, Margarete. Becky Richardson, who was a niece of
Joann's, was there, as were Joann's two daughters, Amber
and Brittany, and Tom Albanese, her ex-husband.

"The previous evening we had requested one of our
other detectives, Detective Rosenberg, to go to the residence and place seals on it because information we learned
late on the 22nd caused us some concern about the possibility that there may be foul play involved," Hanna said.

"The day we arrived, on the 23rd, Dollie Wells presented
me with the items—the license plate, papers, titles, and stuff
like that that they had found inside John Edwards's vehicle, and she had relayed the information to me the previous
afternoon of what she had found, and that's what had caused
our concern," Hanna said.

The crime-scene seals on the house were broken by
Ruffino, and the trio went inside to investigate. Ruffino
and Brotherson had been with the Las Vegas police for
more than twenty years each. Ruffino is one of the most
respected forensic investigators in Las Vegas.

"My duties as crime-scene analyst include taking photographs, dusting for prints, recovering evidence, perform-
ing fingerprint comparisons, crime-scene diagrams, and
basically anything that involves the investigation from a
crime-scene aspect and processing," Ruffino said.

The investigators did not see anything really out of
order at all in the upscale northwest Las Vegas home.

"Basically, that there was nothing out of order, nothing appeared unusual," Hanna said. "The master bedroom
suite, the bed was unmade, but it didn't look anything out
of normal living condition."

Crime-scene investigator Ruffino took photos throughout the house. He took photos of the bedrooms, closets, and drawers.

"I proceeded to take photographs showing various areas of the residence and searched for any type of apparent crime scene at that location," he said.

He closely scrutinized the master bedroom and drawers where Joann's belongings had been left behind, then retrieved by the family. He saw evidence that a man had been living in the home.

"There were items, male possessions, in different areas of the room," Ruffino said. "There was a terry-cloth robe on the floor next to the bed, a man's dress shirt hanging in the closet, and apparently a man's-type T-shirt in the dresser of that room."

"There was a partial roll of Scotch brand mailing-type tape, and that was located on top of the master bedroom . . . bathroom counter," Ruffino said. "I did not get any latents off that particular item."

One thing in the home that definitely stood out for investigators was a cleaning-supply box with cleaning supplies in it that was found lying in the hallway outside of Joann's master bedroom. The box contained a can of Pledge and a dust rag. It appeared as if someone had been cleaning.

"There were cleaning supplies that were left out on top of the hallway stairs, and there was also a furniture polish can I believe at the base of the stairs that was left out, being sort of odd possessions for a well-kept residence," Ruffino said.

"I recovered . . . the partial roll of tape, Scotch brand. I impounded that, and also a Beringer bottle," Ruffino said.

"It was inside of the refrigerator on the first floor of the residence."

The wine bottle proved to have a single latent print on it, which Ruffino lifted. Other than the print, a roll of packing tape, the odd placement of the cleaning supplies, and the family's report of Joann's belongings having been left behind, there was no evidence of a crime at Joann's house.

"Immediately after we left the residence, we went to the impound lot to inspect and process the vehicle," Hanna said. "We took photographs, processed for possible latent prints on the vehicle, inspected it for any signs of violence or other evidence [of] a crime."

"I [took] exposed color negatives of a 1984 Ford Ranger pickup truck at that location, showing overall views of the exterior and interior of the vehicle," Ruffino said. "I processed that particular vehicle for latent prints, of which I recovered one latent fingerprint off of the exterior of the driver door handle."

Next, the investigators turned to the residence of Glenn Wilcox. Wilcox, who worked with Addis at 24-Hour Fitness, was shocked to see investigators at his door. They were asking to search the residence because John Edwards and his girlfriend were missing. Wilcox immediately let the investigators inside.

"It was pretty weird," Wilcox said. "I never had dealt with anything like that before."

"He admitted us into the residence and directed us to the room where Mr. Edwards had apparently stored his property and advised us that Mr. Edwards had not paid him any type of rent and had just moved in approximately a week or so ago," Hanna said.

"Once they got in his room they spent a good afternoon there," Wilcox said. "The detective and forensics guy [were] looking for fingerprints. We talked a little bit and he kind of told me John disappeared and Joann went with him."

Hanna was a little surprised at what he saw in Edwards's room. All of Edwards's stuff was right there in one room. He didn't have a lot of belongings, and it looked as if he was mostly packed up and ready to go. Edwards's computer was packed up, and other items seemed as if they'd been stored away so that they could be easily removed.

"For the most part, the items appeared to be packed up as if he may anticipate leaving, or that he had never really unpacked after arriving there," Hanna said. "Stuff was very neat and orderly, tidy. There was no apparent sleeping arrangement other than a foam workout mat as you'd see at a health club somewhere.

"We started looking through the room and we initially began looking at the property trying to find out someone we could contact with regard to who he may be," Hanna said. "At that point we didn't know who was responsible or why anyone was gone. Just that it didn't seem right."

Hanna found a backpack in the closet. When he inspected it closely, he found a huge hunting knife in a secret location. Hanna tried putting the backpack on and found that the knife was there for a reason. It was concealed in such a way that if someone were to suddenly come upon the individual wearing the backpack, the knife could be accessed quickly and easily.

"I started to think that this guy might be very dangerous if cornered," Hanna said. "To me, it was something I noticed. It was hidden, and as you are dropping the backpack, you don't see the knife until it's there. It's set up so that, if someone says, 'Take your backpack off,' as you are dropping it, the knife comes out. It was in a sheath on the underside of the backpack [and it was] pressing against his back. The thing of it is, it's just a natural movement of dropping the backpack. As your hand comes down, that knife comes right to it. It slides down, and it's already out. You've drawn that knife before anyone ever realizes it's around.

"We are dealing with someone with some serious survivalist instincts," Hanna said.

"Then we started seeing a screenplay that he wrote," Hanna said. "*Purposeful Deceit*. It was nutcase shit. The government against the rest of the world. The government is hiding UFOs and stuff. He was big into them. The government is intentionally hiding them. He'd sent it to Hollywood a lot, trying to get them to pick up on it. This guy seemed like a real conspiracy theorist."

In the room was a significant amount of literature about *Project Blue Book*, the study of UFOs by the U.S. Air Force looking into more than twelve thousand reports of UFOs to try and determine if they could be a threat to national security. Hanna thought the stuff was a little bizarre, but what he found next, though, took the investigation to a new level. In a black duffel bag on the left-hand side of the room were two wallets. The second wallet was completely encased in duct tape.

John Edwards's picture was on multiple identification cards under different names. He looked different in many of the photos. One was for a fitness membership at the Kalispell, Montana, fitness club. Another was a Florida driver's license for a J. Charles Peterson. There was another ID for a John Charles Stone, who was a fitness instructor at Q the Fitness Club in Jacksonville, Florida. Two of the licenses had Cape Coral residences. Another ID appeared to have been stolen from a Salt Lake City man with an Asian name.

"Two wallets were in a bag, and in the first wallet, we found at least four Nevada driver's licenses of other people," Hanna said. "We found a Utah driver's license, a Wisconsin driver's license, health cards from fitness clubs in other states, in other people's names and [with] photographs on them, et cetera.

"The [second] wallet was duct-taped closed," Hanna said. "When we pried it open, there were a . . . bunch of other IDs that he'd been swiping."

But when Hanna sorted through all the items in the second wallet, he also noticed several identification cards in the name of a "John Patrick Addis."

One was a California driver's license. Other IDs were from Alaska.

"I found identifications in the name of John Patrick Addis, and that identification included an Alaska driver's license with a photograph, a California driver's license, an FAA pilot certification license, and an Alaska state instructor verification card in the name of John Addis," Hanna said.

The pictures of the identification of John Addis were shown to Glenn Wilcox, and he said that was the person he knew as John Edwards.

"We found also in his property the materials and packets necessary for making false identification," Hanna said of Addis's possessions. "Not just to include driver's licenses and photo IDs but to include license plate renewal stickers."

Hanna said the Washington license plate "had not been registered to anyone in years, yet this person was manufacturing the little sticker to show that the plate would be current. He was doing so by using a variety of lettering and materials available at most hobby shops.

"We found on his computer a setup . . . he was using to change font size and style to duplicate driver's licenses," Hanna said. "On the driver's license, the state seal will go over a portion of the picture. What we saw was he was using seals and decals from little model car kits to superimpose over a picture to make very qualified-looking identification."

Hanna's mind was racing now. Two people were missing. Joann was an honest, hardworking woman who would never leave her kids alone. Her boyfriend, on the other hand, had apparently been living a lie for months in Las Vegas as "John Edwards" when his real name seemed to be John Addis. He had a backpack with a hidden knife, and this was an individual who appeared to be extremely adept at making false identification cards and assuming fake identities and living under them for lengths of time. It was clear the John Edwards name was a total lie meant to cover who he really was.

"Oh shit," Hanna said. "We've got a problem here."

16 . . . YAVAPAI COUNTY

Gordon Diffendaffer worked for thirty-two years as a detective with the Yavapai County Sheriff's Office in Arizona before retiring recently.

"I guess what I liked most about law enforcement was the variety," Diffendaffer said. "Each case was always at least a little different than the others, and you never knew what tomorrow would bring. It was rarely boring. I also enjoyed the freedom to go wherever I needed to go to conduct my investigations."

Diffendaffer worked criminal investigations, primarily major cases, throughout his career. On August 23, 1995, at 3:45 p.m. he was dispatched to a possible crime scene. The location was Little Hell Canyon.

"I was notified that one of our patrol officers, a Sergeant Parkingson, had responded to that location in response to a complainant notifying him that there was an abandoned vehicle in rather suspicious circumstances at that location," Diffendaffer said.

Just off a roughly fifty-mile stretch of highway that sought to connect Prescott and Ash Fork, Little Hell Canyon is a remote, wickedly hot spot in the summertime, though it can get cold as hell in the winter.

"The nearest town from [where the vehicle was found] would probably be Ash Fork . . . seventeen miles north," Diffendaffer said.

"When I arrived, Sergeant Parkingson and Deputy Bollard were at that location already," Diffendaffer said. "I saw a gold ninety-three Honda Accord parked at the back side of a small lake that's referred to as Little Hell Canyon. The vehicle was approximately a quarter mile off of the main highway, which is Highway 89, and was pretty much at the end of a real rough little two-track dirt road, not the type of road that you would normally travel in that type of a vehicle. The car was pulled into a small clearing that was only barely big enough for the vehicle, and like I said, pretty much at the end of that little road.

"The road actually turns a little to the left and then kind of dead ends in some juniper trees and bushes," Diffendaffer said, adding that only a part of the car could be seen upon approaching from the road.

"The vehicle was locked. The windows were up. We were unable to see any bodies or anything like that in the vehicle. We couldn't see any keys in the vehicle. No damage. The rear seat was the type that folds forward and basically extends the size of the trunk so that you can push the seat forward and get into the trunk area.

"The rear seat was approximately halfway forward, and

from outside the vehicle, that obscured some of the view of the floor of the backseat and the seat itself," Diffendaffer said. "It allowed us to see a portion of the trunk and probably not in the backseat, but we couldn't be for sure what was in the backseat.

"I took an eight millimeter video at the scene," Diffendaffer said.

Diffendaffer could tell the vehicle hadn't been there long.

"When a vehicle sits there for a period of time, you'll get kind of an accumulation of dust on the tires or below the tires," Diffendaffer said. "You know, the weeds appear to have been bent over where the vehicle had run over, and [the grass blades] hadn't straightened out totally, and various things like that. And there wasn't an accumulation of dust on the top of the vehicle like you would find on something sitting out. Down in Arizona it's real dusty, and if a vehicle sits out for maybe even a week, it will have a noticeable coating of dust on it, and this vehicle didn't.

"Because the vehicle was locked, and there was a possibility of it raining again, I had our county fleet management unit respond with a roll-back truck, and they loaded the vehicle onto the truck and took it to Prescott for impound, to be processed," Diffendaffer said.

Diffendaffer ran the tags, and it came back as registered to Joann Albanese of Las Vegas. Information had been entered into a national police computer system a day earlier identifying Joann Albanese as an endangered missing person. Diffendaffer immediately got on the phone with Las Vegas police and was put in touch with Detective Larry Hanna. Hanna learned that the vehicle was found around the time he was searching through "John Edwards's" stuff but was dismayed to learn that there was no sign of either Edwards or Joann at the site of the car. Hanna informed Diffendaffer of the facts, and both men agreed the vehicle would need to be examined as a possible crime scene.

"We got the call that Yavapai County had found her car," Hanna said. "Oh shit. They described it as intentionally hidden, deep in a wooded area of the desert. There was a body of water nearby. . . . So we're still trying to figure out, what the hell is going on?"

The next day, Diffendaffer got a search warrant from a Prescott Justice Court judge. The vehicle was searched at the Yavapai County Fleet Management Center in Prescott.

"Upon searching the vehicle, we found two pillows that were located on the backseat, which was leaning forward from the trunk area," Diffendaffer said. "We found a brown blanket that was also on the back of the seat. We found miscellaneous papers on the seat portion of the backseat itself. We found a brochure from Westcare Runaway Shelter Youth Emergency Services in a pocket behind the driver's seat. We found miscellaneous cards and papers in the console.

"We found a New Mexico–Arizona road map between the passenger seat and the console and an address book with miscellaneous papers between the passenger's seat and the console," the detective said. "We recovered a juniper needle off of the blanket in the trunk, and we recovered a blanket in the trunk that the needle was on.

"We recovered a hand towel in the trunk, sunglasses, and [a] console briefcase in the trunk, and a travel drink bottle on the front floor of the front passenger side, and we recovered a cassette tape that was in the tape deck,"

Diffendaffer said. "At that time, [two crime-scene analysts] and I were the ones processing the car."

The investigators searched for evidence of homicide but found no blood stains or bodily fluids, and with Las Vegas police now fearing the worst, it was decided the lake near where the car was found should be searched. If Addis killed Joann and drove her car to the remote spot in Arizona, it seemed likely Joann's body would be in the area. Unless he dumped the body in the desert on the way to Arizona, it would likely be in the area, because if he left the area on foot, he wouldn't be carrying the body with him.

Investigators, however, although suspicious, were still not sure if Joann was dead.

"I made contact with our sheriff's office dive team, and they searched the lake for bodies," Diffendaffer said. "We found no bodies in the lake. The team captain and three other members. Four people, and I was assisting as I could. It was so shallow that our dive team was able to walk in the water feeling for a body because it was so murky.

"And then we also had members of our backcountry team, which is a volunteer search-and-rescue team, and myself search the area immediately around the lake for approximately, oh, [one] hundred yards from the lake out on each side all the way around the lake, and we found nothing. And then later, our forest patrol officer sergeant and a deputy, along with sixty-one volunteers on foot and horseback, searched an area from milepost 351.5 on Highway 59, where there's a small dirt road that takes off of the highway, over to a pipeline, and then the pipeline access road comes down almost exactly where the vehicle was recovered. They searched that entire area for any type of evidence and found nothing. It was pretty much a massive search."

They found nothing.

Nothing at all.

17 . . . INVESTIGATION

With no sightings of Joann Albanese or "John Edwards" anywhere, and no activities on Joann's credit card or bank accounts, Larry Hanna started to think that Joann Albanese was dead. As he waited and hoped for a miracle, he set about interviewing Joann's close friends. Hanna also set about learning more about his victim and "John Edwards," whom he suspected may have killed Joann in her home, fled in her car, dumped the body—possibly in Little Hells Canyon in Arizona—and then thumbed it to the Mexican border.

Hanna interviewed Joann's family members and close friends, and they all were very clear in saying something was definitely not right. Her car was in Arizona, and no one had heard anything from her. Her boyfriend, whom witnesses said was obsessive and controlling, was missing, and the two disappeared on the night Tara Rivera said Joann was going to dump "John Edwards." The accounts from Rivera were troubling in particular. She described Edwards as a person who had quickly weaseled his way into Joann's life and then controlled everything about her and benefited from her money.

"Joann was very independent and very outspoken," Hanna said. "I talked to her ex-husband, and she had no problem going right up in your face if she had a problem with you. She had a good job at the MGM. Not just room reservations but administration assistance. She had a job, she liked it, and she had her weekends free because the kids would stay in town with dad."

Hanna felt very sorry for Joann's family—in particular her two young daughters and her ex-husband, who was left behind to pick up the pieces after a devastating event in the lives of his children.

"Tom was a real nice, mild-mannered guy," Hanna said. "I empathized with Tom. The girls were having a tough time. They'd been living with their mom, now Mom's gone, they are living with their dad, and no one knows where she is."

If Joann was dead and she'd been murdered by Edwards, it would be an outrageous crime. If this was the scenario that unfolded, it would leave Joann's daughters without their mother. The nature of the crime in and of itself was particularly cruel because the body had apparently been disposed of, leaving the family with no idea of what had actually happened, allowing them no closure.

There was also apparently tension at times in the investigation. Joann's sister was very involved, and rightfully so, but Hanna felt at times Dollie Greenrock Wells needed to slow down and not try to get involved in the police side of the investigation.

"She wouldn't listen," Hanna said. "Always trying to inject herself into the investigation. When we needed information, we'd ask for it. She . . . really caused us some problems."

At this point, Hanna now had evidence that "John Edwards" was really a man by the name of John Patrick Addis. The detective started doing some more digging on that name, and computer records showed he was an ex-felon out of Alaska who had absconded while on parole in California. Since he'd disappeared, no one had shown any interest in tracking him down until he'd showed up in Las Vegas and was subsequently linked to a missing woman. Hanna saw that Addis's felony conviction had come out of Fairbanks, Alaska, and he called the Alaska Department of Corrections. It was then that he learned that Addis was a former Alaska state trooper who'd gone berserk, kidnapped his kids, and gone to prison for it.

Hanna reached out to Addis's family and sisters. The family told him that when Addis was in Michigan, he seemed to many to be the perfect young man.

"John was never a problem child," Hanna said. "Everyone said even when he went to Alaska, they thought he was a great guy. Somehow, suddenly, he became more withdrawn and reclusive and [started] talking about bizarre shit."

Hanna said Addis's family told him that they'd lost all contact with him. They'd wanted to let him know that his father had passed away but had "no place to go to try to tell him."

"They said that since he kidnapped his kids from his first wife in Alaska, and after he did a brief stint in prison, paroled from Fresno, they hadn't heard from him," Hanna recalled. "He dropped off the radar."

Addis's former career as a state trooper concerned Hanna greatly. Hanna now knew he was searching for a man who knew all the tricks Hanna would use to find him. Plus, Addis was apparently very adept at changing his name and manufacturing false identifications. The man had no qualms about living under an assumed name for extended periods of time.

"After Alaska, he got paroled to Fresno, he violated, and just disappeared. He's gone, we don't care, and he went from California to Florida and then worked his way back across [the] country," Hanna said.

Hanna spoke to former Alaska state trooper Jim McCann and learned the even more disturbing information about Addis's expertise in the fields of forensics and crime-scene investigation. He also learned of Addis's previous relationships and contentious divorce and allegations of abuse.

"I think he was very, very controlling," Hanna said. "It's my way, or he might knock the shit out of them."

The Las Vegas detective quickly learned Addis was not an average guy. He was an outdoorsman who could survive off the land, literally, by hunting for his food. He was a bush pilot who could disappear into the wilderness or assume a new identity, and no one would ever be able to find him unless he slipped up.

"When I first heard the name John Patrick Addis, he'd never had any record besides kidnapping," Hanna said. "Kidnapped the kids, flew down, landed in an open field in Montana, and walked off with the kids. Lands the plane in an open field, and he sets up shop [with the kids] like nothing happened.

"Jim, his sergeant, was a pilot," Hanna said. "Well, John

learned how to fly, and in very short order he excelled. . . .
He became one of the best bush pilots you could find in
Alaska. He could set a plane down anywhere, and he had
great skills. He was tough and skilled at being [in] the wilderness. I heard enough from Jim McCann and the others,
that, okay, he's skilled, a survivalist, a hunter, he's a pilot,
and he's very skilled at false identities and how to make
them, generate them, and make them work. He can blend
in anywhere he wants to."

Hanna secured a fingerprint of Addis from when he was
arrested in Montana. The fingerprint was compared to the
fingerprint on the wine bottle from Joann's home, and it
was a match. Hanna now knew for sure that he was dealing
with the elusive John Patrick Addis, and he quickly realized he was going to have his hands full on this one.

"He's going to be a bitch to find," the detective said.
"Fucking James Bond. I'm looking forward to sitting
across the table from him, but you have to understand, he's
someone who's done what you've done. He knows the law.
He knows how cops work. He knows the rules of evidence,
and he's great at manipulating people. Excellent."

Hanna spent the following weeks documenting Addis's
whereabouts before he came to Vegas. He learned Addis
had lived across the country, working at gyms and scam-
ming women he'd met there. He talked to detectives in
Salt Lake and learned about the woman there who'd been
scammed. He talked to Florida detectives and got further
information about the identity scam that allowed Addis
to assume the identity of John Edwards upon leaving the
Cape Coral area. Hanna was beginning to get a very strong
feeling that Joann had been killed.

"Nobody's heard from her," Hanna said. "Very unusual

for her. Meanwhile, every woman [Addis] ever met, he manipulated them."

And, the investigator was becoming more and more convinced Addis had dumped her body in Arizona and thumbed his way into Mexico.

"Well, where did he go?" Hanna said. "There's a two-lane road from where the car was that would take you right into Mexico. A car drive from Prescott, three hours, four hours, maybe. Probably got a ride, hitchhiked, crossed right down there.

"By the time they find the car, he's well into Mexico," Hanna said. "Where else you going to go? You've got no place to go. No family. Nothing working for you but the sweat on the brow and your brain. He had only what he had at the time, which was not a lot."

Hanna also learned that Addis's second wife had remarried and had a summer home in the Prescott area. In fact, several former Alaska State Troopers spent time in the Prescott area on winter vacations. Addis's second wife had divorced him after just four months, and this raised in Hanna's mind the idea that Addis may have known the area because he'd been to Prescott on trips to stalk his ex-wife. The idea of Addis stalking his ex was admittedly speculation, but the short travel distance between the remote location where the car was found and the home of the ex-wife, Sarah Rayder, seemed to be an unlikely coincidence for Hanna. Rayder told detectives she'd not seen Addis in years and wanted absolutely nothing to do with him.

"[She and her new husband] owned a condominium approximately ten minutes from where the vehicle was found," Hanna said.

The detective compiled all the information he had about

the investigation into a report for a possible submission of a murder warrant even though Joann's body was nowhere to be found and he had very little evidence. He summarized his investigation about the investigation into Joann's disappearance, and Addis's whereabouts, in a Las Vegas police report. The following are excerpts:

We were contacted by the family of Joann Albanese regarding the Missing Persons report that had been filed on Joann Albanese on Aug. 20, 1995, by her 16-year-old daughter. When Joann Albanese failed to return home, Amber contacted Thomas Albanese and, subsequently, the Metropolitan Police Department, whereupon the Missing Persons report was filed under event #950820-1858.

Noted in the Missing Person's report were the irregularities that the children had found. The interior garage door [was] unlocked, which was usually kept locked; the bedroom door unlocked, which was habitually kept locked in Joann Albanese's absence; Joann Albanese's bracelet and watch, which she habitually took off only while showering in the bathroom, and her purse, containing credit cards, wallet, etc., [were] still in her bedroom. The residence may have been recently cleaned, as cleaning supplies were left in the upstairs hallway and near the staircase.

There appeared to be nothing else out of order, but the family did note that Joann's boyfriend, John Edwards, [his] vehicle was parked in front of the residence, and Joann Albanese's vehicle was missing. I subsequently learned from Richardson and Wells that Joann was last seen on Saturday, [August] 19th, at approximately 4:30

p.m. by her supervisor at the MGM Grand Hotel-casino where she left work. At approximately six p.m. on the 19th, Joann Albanese called her mother, Greenrock, and during their conversation Joann said she was meeting John Edwards for dinner that evening and said that after several months of dating she felt their relationship was going nowhere; as such, she was going to terminate the relationship.

The family learned that both Joann and John had failed to show up for work at their respective places of employment, nor did they call in to state their reasons for not going to work. No one had contact with them since late Saturday afternoon, early evening.

As this behavior is not unusual for adults who frequently decide to take an unscheduled trip or spend time alone, I requested that the family begin searching Joann Albanese's bedroom and personal belongings for any indication as to where she may go and attempt to find the names and phone numbers of friends who the family could contact in an effort to determine Joann's whereabouts. As well, I asked them to look inside Edwards' vehicle in an effort to determine if there was anything in it that would assist in determining his whereabouts.

Hanna wrote about what was found in the truck and how little was actually known about "John Edwards."

The family's inspection of John's vehicle netted more questions about him due to the documents and items found in the vehicle. I attempted to learn more about

Edwards by running the Florida license plate on his vehicle to determine where he lived in Florida, and found that there was no record of that plate on file with the Florida [Department] of Motor Vehicles. I did the same with the vehicle identification number of the Ford truck, and found a record of a title for the vehicle in the names of Duverny Dumercy, or Robb Wilson, at 1441 Wilton Avenue in Orlando. It showed no current registration.

I learned that the address on the title was located in the Orange County Sheriff's Office jurisdiction. I contacted them requesting they attempt to contact the resident at 1441 Wilton Avenue to determine the identity of the owner of the vehicle known to be used by Edwards. They ultimately provided us the phone number of a Marie Dumercy.

We later contacted the Dumercy family and learned that the vehicle had been sold by the Dumercys in 1993. It had been sold by the father, and they did not know to whom it was sold. The Dumercys did not know the specifics of the transactions, and the father was currently out of the country for an unspecified amount of time. The title found in Edwards' vehicle was signed by the seller in 1993, but no further information regarding the transaction was noted on the title.

The investigator wrote of his contacts with Tara Rivera and Edwards's supervisors at the gyms where he worked. He also recounted how it was learned that Edwards was someone else living under the alias of a man in Cape Coral, Florida.

This, in and of itself, made Albanese's disappearance
suspicious and highly probable that she could be the victim of foul play. As such, Albanese and her vehicle were
entered into NCIC as an endangered missing person.

Hanna described the search through the Albanese
home, Addis's belongings, the multiple identifications, the
physical processing of the Addis truck, and the discovery
of Joann's vehicle in Arizona.

Hanna described his investigation of Addis's former life
as an Alaska state trooper with an investigative background:

Investigators received photographs and fingerprint
information from the Alaska Department of Public
Safety on the subject known as Addis. I also had a
conversation with Paul Keller, of the Fairbanks Alaska
Police Department, who is a past associate of John
Addis. Keller said that if the subject we are looking for
was, in fact, the John Addis he was familiar with, he
knew him to be an ex Alaska state investigator; to be
very intelligent; to be proficient in criminal investigations; was an instructor in homicide and crime scenes;
was an accomplished pilot; skilled at wilderness survival; and an excellent marksman. Keller was not sure
of all the circumstances surrounding Addis's departure
from the Alaska state troopers, but did advise that it was
his personal belief, having known Addis, that if he were
cornered, he would be a very dangerous individual.

Hanna recounted Addis's remarkable travels across the
United States after being released from prison for kidnapping his kids.

Based on information from numerous sources, investigators have pieced together that after leaving the Alaska state police agency, Addis was arrested in Montana in 1987 pursuant to a warrant for parental abduction out of Alaska. In 1988, he was paroled on Interstate compact to Fresno, California, whereupon the parole board lost contact with Addis, and he was listed as a parole violator, but no warrant was issued for his arrest. During this time, Addis was in California, Oregon, and Washington.

Apparently, Addis went to Georgia in 1989; was in Oklahoma in 1990; and in Canada and Arizona, on vacation and trips based on photographic documents obtained, in 1991 and 1992. In 1993, he was in Florida, and later Utah until September of 1994. Addis/ Edwards arrived in Las Vegas in October of 1994, and remained . . . in 1995 until his departure at the time of Albanese's disappearance. While we have made efforts to determine if there had been any similar type of incidents in any aforementioned states, few responses have been received. Another more direct inquiry was ultimately made to specific local and state agencies and the information was entered into the Violent Criminal Apprehension Program with the Federal Bureau of Investigation.

Based on the information learned thus far in the investigation, Edwards/Addis is known to frequent or be employed by fitness centers; often befriends and lives with a local female whom he would meet at one of these fitness centers; plan a future together; and then he would abruptly leave. Addis is capable of adapting new identities by manufacturing identification such as the one he did from the state of Florida with the materials previously noted.

Based on information provided by officers in Alaska, Addis has purportedly befriended women in California and Florida, and subsequently taken money from them. The one incident wherein some verification has been obtained is in Salt Lake City. In Addis's frequent moves from state to state, he has used his true identity, John Addis, but upon leaving Utah, he apparently assumed a new identity. The reason for this has not been established as yet, as there are no known warrants for Addis' arrest, or incidents wherein Addis may be a suspect.

When Addis left Utah, he was purportedly operating a beige pickup, yet upon arriving in Las Vegas, he was riding a motorcycle. Addis' last known vehicle was the blue Ford pickup. It appears that Addis can change vehicles as easily as his identification, and not register them, obtaining old license plates and manufacturing his own renewal stickers, thus leaving no trail for investigators to follow.

While the possibility that Joann Albanese may have left voluntarily with Edwards/Addis was entertained by investigators, the discovery that Edwards/Addis was in fact John Patrick Addis, living in Las Vegas under an assumed identity; the discovery of Albanese's vehicle concealed in a remote area of Arizona; and now the length of time since her disappearance as well as the unlikeliness of her abandoning her two children and other family members with absolutely no contact; abandoning an estimated $40,000 to $50,000 in equity in her home; monthly spousal support payments of $1,000 and child support payments of $1,000; and a long sought-after job, it is apparent to investigators that Joann Albanese's disappearance was not a voluntary one and that John Patrick Addis is not only responsible for her disappearance, but for her apparent murder.

Hanna saw a pattern in the women John Addis targeted. He was looking for women he could take advantage of, and who might be a little bit vulnerable emotionally.

"She was the type of girl John would target," Hanna said about Joann. "She wasn't real slim and statuesque, she wasn't portly, but she did have some reservations about her weight. John would have blond, blue-eyed, gorgeous women throwing themselves at him, and he wasn't interested in them. He looked for women who were reserved, timid, self-esteem wasn't that great, and I think he misread Joann. He got into a situation where she wasn't easily manipulated, and if she didn't like something, you were going to know about it.

"His whole MO is best defined by Joann and the girl in Salt Lake City," Hanna said. "[The woman in Salt Lake] was also a dark-haired woman, and she was going to the gym for physical therapy. He hooked up with her. They were going to get married. They moved into her place. . . . None of the utilities were in his name. She was told they had a shared bank account. Whenever they would need money, they would go to the bank, she would wait in the car, 'I'll go in and take care of it sweetheart, you wait in the car. I'll go take care of it.' Then, he disappeared. She went to the bank and said, 'Let me see about my account.' 'What are you talking about? You have no account. This guy never existed. Whatever he was doing with the money, he wasn't depositing it here.' He always lived behind the woman he could control. If you are looking for John Addis, you won't see John Addis. He won't leave a trail.

"So we have an ex-cop, and now he's showing up here in Las Vegas under an assumed identity and we have a [missing] woman," the detective said. "One of the things I was looking for in the past was, are there any other dead women out there?"

Hanna came to conclude that Addis likely murdered Joann at her home during an argument. He was a strong man, and he would have known how to kill her without leaving any evidence behind. It's all speculation, but Hanna suspects she was likely choked or strangled and then dumped in Arizona. The murder, Hanna believes, was not planned, because Addis left all his possessions behind in his apartment.

"I believe she was killed here in Las Vegas, in her bedroom," Hanna said. "Strangulation or broken neck probably given John's strength and his expertise.

"I think Joann got up in his face, and he wasn't thinking on this one," the detective said. "This was something he was not thinking through. If he'd have been thinking . . . we wouldn't have found all his shit at the apartment. If he'd have been thinking, that stuff would have been long gone. Absent a single fingerprint on a wine bottle in the refrigerator that returned to John Addis and that envelope in the truck and the stuff found in his room, we wouldn't have known who he was. And, keep in mind, that truck was a dead end. Some guy in Florida says, 'Oh yeah, I sold that to some guy five years ago.' The plate, a Washington plate, was a dead end. It came back to nothing.

"Had he gone back to that room and had he grabbed his backpack and the stuff he had in there, there would have been no holding him back," Hanna said. "It would have taken us a lot longer to deal with him. One print off a wine bottle in her refrigerator. It came back to him."

The detective knew it was going to be very, very difficult to find Addis if, in fact, he had gone to Mexico.

"Keep in mind, he can make up any story he wants to and who's going to refute it?" Hanna said. "He finds an American or somebody sympathetic to Americans in Mexico and he can say, 'Hey, I got beat up and robbed; can you help me with a place to stay until I can get on my feet? Hey, I've done training, I've done this.' Gets settled in, gets a job, and gets himself set up and starts all over again."

With those facts in mind, Hanna headed to the Clark County District Attorney's Office to get a warrant for murder. He knew it would be a tough sell, and he initially faced resistance. There was no body and no crime scene, he was told, but he eventually found a champion of the case.

Her name is Abbi Silver.

18 . . . GUADALAJARA

In 1996, a Caucasian man walked into a Gold's Gym in downtown Guadalajara, Mexico, and introduced himself as John Stone. He was big and strong, with blond hair, and he was charismatic. He told the gym's employees he was a personal trainer of wealthy individuals in the United States who might want to work out and even join the gym. The gym staffers let this visitor, "John Stone," who went by the name "Juan Carlos," sample the exercise equipment and get in a good workout.

An American who worked as a manager at the gym, Stevie Harlingen,* showed up for work a short time later. He wondered who the man was and was told he was a fitness trainer for the wealthy. An investigator with the U.S. Consulate Office in Guadalajara later interviewed Harlingen about his encounter with "John Stone."

"One day, in approximately late 1996, Harlingen entered the gym in Guadalajara and saw a white male working out," investigators wrote of their interview with Harlingen. "He had not previously seen this individual and inquired who he was. He was informed the man was not a gym member, but he'd convinced personnel to allow him to enter and use the facilities, claiming to be the personal trainer of various wealthy individuals he hoped to bring to the gym. The man, known as John Stone, was allowed to exercise at the gym without ever purchasing a membership."

Harlingen started talking to Stone, and Stone told him he was thirty-eight. He identified himself as a weight-training and tennis coach from Minnesota. Stone said he had been a professional cross-country skier until he suffered a serious injury. He also claimed to be a former police officer and writer, and he volunteered to assist Harlingen in writing a novel.

"Harlingen described Stone as having a strong build and said that he was a very friendly individual," authorities would later write. "Even though his Spanish was minimal, Stone would loudly greet everyone in the gym each time he arrived. Harlingen also said Stone was well read. On one occasion, after an earthquake, Stone spoke at length explaining how plates shift, causing tremors, and how mountains are formed as a result of an underground movement."

Harlingen heard from his friend and fellow Gold's Gym employee, Alberto Humberto Abreau,* that Stone was having multiple sexual encounters with women. He kept a huge box of condoms in his flat for sex. At one point, Stone asked Harlingen and Abreau to pay his rent, telling them he would pay them back in women.

"He [offered] to invite women over to the apartment for Harlingen and Abreau for exchange in the payment of rent," investigators wrote. "Stone said they could have wonderful parties, not only due to the women he would provide, but also due to his expertise as a chef."

Harlingen informed Stone he was married and rejected the offer as ridiculous. Harlingen thought the action was bizarre, but his encounters with Stone got even more bizarre a month later when he had a conversation with Stone about space. Stone revealed to Harlingen he was a believer in aliens and that, one day, the aliens would be coming to earth to retrieve their human offspring.

"Stone commented that humans had been sent here from other planets, each race with a specific mission to perform," FBI investigators later wrote. "Caucasians, according to Stone, were the offspring of extraterrestrials, having been procreated with aliens."

Harlingen was startled by the comments when he realized that Stone "was completely serious." Investigators wrote that Stone "even offered to take Harlingen to New Mexico, where much alien activity takes place, saying 'conversations could be monitored' and space vehicles could actually be seen, thus verifying the existence of these creatures and the cooperation of the U.S. government in allowing them to function and in maintaining their secrecy."

Stone told Harlingen that American military pilots were sometimes made available to these aliens for various reasons.

"He said that if a flight disappears, it's frequently because the pilot has been taken by life-forms from other planets with the blessing of government officials," Harlingen recalled.

Harlingen immediately concluded Stone was, at the

very least, "very strange." He went home that night and
told his wife about the out-of-the-ordinary conversation.

"Something's wrong with him," he said.

Alberto Humberto Abreau owns a small door-manufacturing
shop in Guadalajara. He met John Stone at another gym
in Guadalajara, Lyon's Gym, in late 1996 or early 1997
and almost immediately found the American to be likable. Stone was very friendly and outgoing, and Stone
lived not too far from the gym, approximately two blocks
from Calle Mazamitla in the city. The apartment Stone was
living in was just down the street from a small grocery
store.

Abreau came to like Stone very much. Stone talked
about being a former ski instructor from Michigan with
ties to Alaska. He also talked a lot about women and loving Mexico. He said he'd had a dispute with his family and
had decided to leave America for a while. Stone was also
a writer, and he never had any money. Abreau often gave
Stone some cash so he could buy food. Feeling sorry for
him, Abreau let Stone move into his place of business on
Calle Virgen, in Guadalajara. Stone later moved into a residence owned by a friend of Abreau's. The eighty-year-old
man owned the flat near Plaza Patria in Guadalajara. The
building was vacant, and Stone lived there alone.

"He said he'd lived in Alaska for some time," Abreau
recalled for FBI officials. "Stone said he was of Finnish
ancestry. He spoke a little Finnish and was able to speak
some Spanish as well. Stone worked as a tennis instructor.
He also taught English and gave piano lessons."

FBI officials learned from Abreau that Stone's "financial

state was desperate. He never had any money, and Abreau would sometimes make available small amounts of cash to Stone for food purchases. Abreau was teaching wrestling classes at Gold's Gym and introduced Stone to Gold's Gym as well."

The small-business owner told authorities Stone was very, very active in dating local women from Guadalajara. At one point, he dated a single mother in Guadalajara who managed a hardware store, but the relationship ended when the woman dumped Stone. He also knew Stone had dated another woman with the last name of Guerrero.

Stone struck Abreau as an extremely intelligent individual who kept himself in very good shape and worked out extensively. Abreau was impressed with his ability to survive in a foreign city with no money.

"He was well read and interested in various subjects, including astronomy," Abreau told authorities. "He was a believer in the existence of extraterrestrial life-forms and frequently spoke on this subject."

Another person who met "John Stone" in Guadalajara around the same time was Adalia Guerrero.* Guerrero is a very attractive woman who lives in Cihuatlán, Jalisco, Mexico. She was about thirty when she met John Stone through a mutual friend in March of 1996. He said he was thirty-eight, and she dated him for several months until she ended the relationship out of fear. He was relentless in insisting she marry him. When she rebuffed his constant requests, he became violent and scared her.

Later, she heard that Stone had started dating another woman, Laura Liliana Casillas Padilla. Guerrero said when she dated Stone, "He used the name of John Charles Stone Peterson" and went by the name "Juan Carlos."

She saw Stone as a handsome older man who was very physically fit, and he was a romantic. He said he was a ski instructor from Minnesota, and he quickly swept her off her feet. The couple started dating, and during the first three months, she said he was very romantic to her.

"He began to write a novel, and the novel was a story of their romance together," investigators would later summarize. "Guerrero remembers that the manuscript was about two hundred pages long. She went to the post office and mailed it to fifteen or twenty publishers in the United States. One publisher wrote back to say that they were interested, but Guerrero can't recall any of the details."

John Stone was living at the time for free in a small flat owned by an eighty-year-old man from Guadalajara. Stone never had any money at all, but he did have a computer and a guitar. Shortly after Stone and Guerrero started to date, Stone suggested they get married. Guerrero didn't want to be married to Stone, yet he was persistent.

"She continued to refuse to marry him, and his temperament changed," FBI officials wrote of Guerrero's description of Addis. "He would become very moody and at times would sob; then he would become very romantic."

"He tried to keep me away from friends and family, and he became angry when I went out alone with my mother," Guerrero said.

Guerrero told authorities her new boyfriend was obsessed with the concept of alien life. He also wanted to handle all her money for her.

"On one occasion, he almost hit [me] while walking in

the park, but [I] threatened to call the police and he backed down," Guerrero recalled. "He became angry when I wouldn't let him make plans with my money from my job."

Guerrero told authorities "John Stone" worked out daily and took long bike rides. He often slept in parks. He gave tennis lessons and taught English to children. Stone talked frequently of wanting to open and manage a gym.

"He hated hot weather and spoke of wanting to see the state of Chiapas in Mexico," Guerrero said. "He knew how to play the guitar and the piano. He seemed very well read and spoke of the pyramids in Egypt. He [spoke of] medicine, unidentified [flying] objects, and Area 51. He claimed to be a doctor or paramedic in the United States."

"John Stone" had a tendency of whistling songs so loudly that he could be heard several houses away. The man always carried a small Swiss Army knife in his front pocket and a Spanish/English dictionary in his back pocket.

"He claimed he had a brother that fought in the first Persian Gulf war," Guerrero told investigators. "He explained how soldiers would inject themselves with drugs between their toes so as not to have needle marks."

Guerrero increasingly found her boyfriend's behavior bizarre, threatening, and controlling. His behavior was starting to scare her. She broke it off with him—and he was not happy. Then, on January 3, 1997, when she left Guadalajara to go to Cihuatlán for the holidays, someone broke into both her home and her brother's home.

The only things taken from the home were pictures. The thief did not force any locks or windows. Guerrero was convinced "John Stone" had perpetrated the break-in or paid someone to carry it out.

Miguel Casillas Rosales is the proud father of Laura Liliana Casillas Padilla. He described his daughter to U.S.
Consulate authorities as an intelligent and loving young
woman who was very close to her mother, her sisters, and
her brothers. Casillas is an engineer by trade and manages
an engineering firm in Guadalajara. His daughter Laura
Liliana worked at the engineering firm.

Casillas first came to know "John Stone" when Laura
Liliana showed up at their home with Stone in tow. Stone
was much older than Laura Liliana, and so Casillas didn't
imagine the two were involved in anything more serious
than a friendship. Laura Liliana and one of her brothers
had come to know Stone at a Gold's Gym in Guadalajara.
Stone was apparently somewhat down on his luck and living as a vagabond. He said he'd been a ski instructor in
Minnesota and decided to get away. He was also a writer,
but everyone noticed he never had any money. He was very
kind and outgoing, and Laura Liliana had invited Stone
over to the family home in Guadalajara for dinner.

Slowly, Casillas saw more of Stone with his daughter.
He still didn't take the matter too seriously because Stone
seemed to him to be at least fifteen years older than his
twenty-five-year-old daughter, and he didn't want to make
too much of it. Witness statements Casillas gave to authorities seem to indicate Casillas thought his daughter's contacts with Stone were more of a friendship than a romance.
His daughter was a grown woman, and he did not want to
pry, but over time, he noticed Stone showing up at more
and more family events.

"Stone visited Laura Liliana's parents' home two or

three times," FBI officials wrote. "He also attended parties at Mr. Casillas's engineering firm and once went with the Casillas family to a cabin they own in the mountains of Jalisco, in the town of Mazamitla. Mr. Casillas said that Stone was much older than his daughter and, therefore, did not believe that their dating was very serious."

Witness statements and documents from Las Vegas police files indicate the Casillas family is a warm and loving family, and they also were apparently willing to trust an American and welcome him into their lives and invite him into their home. After all, Stone seemed to be a very kind man to them. He seemed to care about Laura Liliana, and he was very outgoing. He was an enjoyable person to be around. One picture of Addis and Laura Liliana together shows them sitting at a picnic table. Both are smiling. The Casillas family, from a distance, was apparently disarmed by Addis and had no reason whatsoever to believe that Laura Liliana had actually been befriended by a facade of a human being. A shadow. A killer. A specter of a person with a long history of causing chaos, sadness, and misery. There were no immediate signs that Laura Liliana was, in reality, in the presence of an extremely dangerous man.

A predator.

19 ... ONE STEP AHEAD

Las Vegas police detective Larry Hanna did everything he could in the weeks and months after the disappearance of Joann Albanese and John Addis to find them. He sent hundreds of fliers to police agencies across the United States. They read:

**LAS VEGAS METROPOLITAN POLICE
DEPARTMENT**

**Missing
Wanted for Questioning**

**John Patrick Addis [with three photos]
Joann H. Albanese [with one photo]**

Our agency is investigating the disappearance of Joann Albanese, along with her boyfriend, John Addis.

Addis had been living in the Las Vegas area since 1994 under the assumed name John H. Edwards. Albanese's vehicle was found outside Prescott, Arizona, and investigators believe Addis knows her whereabouts. Addis is a former Alaska state trooper, skilled investigator, pilot, survivalist and marksman; can manufacture false identification; known to frequent or be employed at fitness centers. Addis is known to have been in California, Washington, Georgia, Oklahoma, Canada, Arizona, Florida, Utah, Nevada and New Mexico.

Hanna sent the police flier to every law enforcement agency in the country. A press release was distributed to the media as well, and media exposure became a significant strategy in the investigation, largely with the assistance of the Albanese family. Joann's sister, Dollie Greenrock Wells, was instrumental as well in getting the story in both the local and national news and keeping it there.

"We believed that nationwide exposure was essential to locating Addis," Hanna said. "Flyers with photographs of both Addis and Albanese, physical descriptions, a history of cities or states where Addis was known to have resided, as well as a cover letter explaining the nature of our investigation were prepared and distributed not only locally, but to the state county and law enforcement agencies where Addis was believed to have been. In October 1995, the same fliers and cover letters were sent to every state-level investigative agency in the United States. The family placed the fliers and information about Albanese and Addis on the Internet. Few responses were received other than verification of information already learned by investigators."

Hanna was sure Addis was in Mexico. He wrote as much in a 1996 police report:

Believing that a logical action by Addis would be to continue south from where Albanese's vehicle was abandoned and enter Mexico, in November 1995, investigators translated the fliers and sent them, along with copies of the fliers [in English], to 135 hotels and resorts, that may have health clubs, along the Pacific Coast of Mexico, commonly referred to as the Mexican Riviera. No leads or additional information resulted from these fliers.

The press releases did generate a great deal of interest in Las Vegas. The *Las Vegas Review-Journal* picked up the story, told of the disappearance, and later did a lengthy feature story on Addis and his background. Television stations broadcast a photo of Joann Albanese and Addis taken during their trip to Hawaii. Addis, in the photo, is leaning to his right, with his arm around Joann, and both are smiling.

Tara Rivera was watching the local television news in Las Vegas a few days after she'd last talked to Joann Albanese when she saw a special report on the disappearance. A Las Vegas woman was missing, and so was her boyfriend. They showed Joann's photo, along with the photo of John Edwards, and Rivera knew the chances of ever seeing her friend again were very slim. She learned that Edwards was not who he'd said he was—that he was a former Alaska state trooper named John Patrick Addis—and she figured immediately that it was at least probable that the man she'd introduced to Joann had killed her. She would feel very guilty over this fact for years, but she has since come to terms with the reality that she'd encountered a master con man. There was just no way she could have known that "Edwards" was actually a predator of women he met at gyms.

"It was terrible," she said.

Brenda Ulrich was deeply shaken by the disappearance of her friend. The two had had a falling out over Ulrich's husband being the best man at the wedding of Joann's former boyfriend. Ulrich had called Joann and left a voice message for her, seeing if the two could patch things up. She never heard back from Joann.

"The next thing I knew, I saw it on the news, and it was devastating," Ulrich said.

Eli Koch was greatly grieved over the disappearance of her longtime friend as well. She'd returned from a trip to Brazil in August of 1995 and was planning to go out to lunch with Joann upon her return. Shortly after she got home, though, she learned Joann and her boyfriend, "John Edwards," were missing, and that John Edwards wasn't his real name. Koch called and talked to Joann's mother, offering comfort to the grief-stricken and worried woman.

"I had to call her," Koch said.

Margarete Greenrock would live the remainder of her life in sadness over the disappearance of her daughter. She would later tell authorities she wouldn't let herself believe that her daughter was dead.

"She had five thousand dollars income a month,"

Greenrock said. "She was a talented girl on computers at MGM, and she was a travel consultant, and she . . . would never, never, never leave me without telling me. She didn't even have a fingernail fixed without telling me. She would call and say, 'Mom, don't worry. I'm going for an hour, hour and a half. I'm having my fingernail fixed.'

"I don't want to believe that something happened," Greenrock said. "I believe she's somewhere."

Joann's daughters and her ex-husband at first hoped the matter would be resolved quickly, but with time, it became apparent that the cruel mystery of what happened to Joann was not going to be solved—at least not right away. Those who are close to the family have said the loss of Joann has been forever life-altering for her two girls. Tom Albanese, they said, has kept the family together and does his best to pick up the pieces with no resolution as to what exactly happened.

The Albanese family denied a request for an interview through their daughter, Amber, but the public record shows that the family was actively involved in trying to find Joann. Joann's sister, Dollie Greenrock Wells, was a leader in this regard, working tirelessly to secure publicity for her sister's disappearance. Wells was not going to rest until her sister was found. She would later tell the *Las Vegas Review-Journal* the tragedy of losing Joann had a profound impact on her family.

"My mother has never been the same physically or mentally," Wells said. "She will not leave the house, and she is always hoping. She is still holding out hope, and she has a shrine in her home with the pictures," Wells said.

Wells said the knowledge that Addis is still out there is a nagging torture that never dissipates. "I know who did this is still walking around out there, and that is what really makes me mad," she said.

"The person who did this should be punished, and if I could do it myself without being prosecuted, I would. That's how angry you still feel."

There was no activity on any of Joann's credit cards in the months after her disappearance. A police check showed no income reported to the Social Security Administration. Wells, meanwhile, was very successful in getting Joann's disappearance on national television. In March of 1996, the nationally syndicated television program *A Current Affair* aired the story of Albanese's disappearance. Subsequent to this airing, detectives received a few leads about the missing couple but none panned out. In April 1996, Wells and police got the story on the television show *Unsolved Mysteries*. The show has since aired a piece on the disappearance of Joann and Addis more than a dozen times.

"We did do a special bulletin on Addis in 1996," said Courtney Ennis, an employee of the production company that produces the show. "We did then do a larger package on the case for Lifetime Television, and it aired numerous times."

No concrete leads were ever uncovered despite the repeated airing of the program, but news of the show's first broadcast, in 1996, urging people to provide tips on Addis's whereabouts, reached all the way back to Fairbanks, Alaska, where local columnist Dermit Cole wrote about it briefly in the *Fairbanks Daily News-Miner* after contacting Jim McCann.

"*The Stranger Beside Me*," Cole wrote. "Those are the words of retired Alaska State Trooper Sergeant Jim McCann to describe John Addis, who worked together with McCann in the 1970s in Alaska. A story about Addis, fifty-one, was included in an episode of *Unsolved Mysteries* on

TV Monday. Before he turned to crime, Addis taught law enforcement personnel about crime scene analysis and was a talented investigator. He is wanted now in connection with the death of a Las Vegas woman."

All of his old friends in Alaska knew Addis had gone crazy and was a convicted felon, but the news that he had been linked to the disappearance of a Las Vegas woman was still disturbing though not completely surprising.

"I guess I wasn't too terribly surprised," Paul Bartlett said. "I knew he was nuts and going more nuts.

"Again, no one really understood how deeply distressed he was," Bartlett said. "I guess you could surmise that he was really on a bad road, but as far as murdering goes, it wouldn't bother him to kill somebody. It's just because of how he looked at it in killing an animal. I don't think, in looking back at everything, I don't think it would really bother him."

Gail McCann said news of the disappearance "spread like wildfire" through the circles of people who knew Addis. She, for one, was completely stunned that anyone she'd known could be accused of murder.

"Everyone was stunned," she said. "Speechless. Jaw-dropping-down-to-your-knees speechless."

Jim McCann was saddened to see what had happened to Joann's family, and he was willing to help in any way he could. Dollie Greenrock Wells, he said, often called him for information on Addis and what he was like. She also provided regular updates on the search for Addis and her sister.

What happened next would be the closest anyone would ever come to catching John Patrick Addis. His ability to slip away from arrest and justice in 1997 can only be described as a great error combined with incredible luck for Addis.

The moment unfolded after an airing of a segment in

March 1997 on the *Geraldo* television show about the dis-
appearances of Addis and Albanese. The story recounted
how Addis had been a state trooper, was sent to prison in
Alaska, and then was linked to the disappearance of Joann
in Las Vegas in 1995. Throughout the show, the mustachioed
Geraldo—perhaps most famous for uncovering Al Capone's
empty vault of treasures—urged viewers to call in if they had
any information on the whereabouts of either Addis or Joann.

Surprisingly, a single caller called in to the show's tip
line and reported a sighting of Addis. The caller said Addis
was working at a Gold's Gym in Guadalajara. The tip
seemed credible. The caller had specific information about
the man at the gym, who sounded very much like Addis.
The producers of the show immediately called Las Vegas
police detectives Larry Hanna and Ray Brotherson. The
two were out of town, so they called Joann's sister, Dollie
Greenrock Wells, next.

"My partner and I, Ray Brotherson, were out of town at
the time, in Montana, on another murder caper—a missing
persons/murder," Hanna said. "Well, we didn't react quick
enough, so Dollie cold-called the gym in Guadalajara and
asked for him by name."

Stevie Harlingen was sleeping at home in Guadalajara
when his phone rang at 1 a.m. The person on the other end
of the line was a woman. He was a little perturbed that
someone would call so late at night. He could tell she was
an American. The woman on the phone was asking him
about "John Edwards" at Gold's Gym. Harlingen politely
informed the woman there was no "John Edwards" who
worked at the gym in Guadalajara.

"Harlingen responded he had no employee by that name and had no American employees at all," FBI investigators would later summarize in reports. "The woman insisted he was lying, and that Edwards worked at Gold's."

Harlingen said the only person he knew who fit the description offered by the unidentified woman over the phone was a man he knew as "John Stone," but Stone was not an employee. Instead, he just worked out at the gym.

"As Stone was described, the woman said they were talking about the same person, but that his true name was John Edwards," investigators wrote of the incident.

Harlingen asked who the woman was, and she said she was an old girlfriend of John Edwards.

"Harlingen mentioned Stone was thirty-eight, and the woman immediately corrected him, saying he was much older," investigators wrote. "The caller then commented that she was a former girlfriend of Edwards who was interested in getting back together with him."

The woman told Harlingen not to tell Stone she'd called and said she would recontact him at 2 p.m. the next day. Harlingen thought the whole thing was bizarre. The next morning, John Stone walked into Gold's Gym, where Harlingen was working. Stone was with his new girlfriend, Laura Liliana Casillas Padilla, and Harlingen mentioned the bizarre call the night before.

"One of your old girlfriends called me last night," Harlingen said.

Stone seemed largely uninterested in the comment.

"She said your name is John Edwards," Harlingen said.

Stone stopped, turned around, and glared at Harlingen with a wild look in his eyes.

"Immediately, his eyes widened, and his expression

changed," Harlingen recalled for investigators. "He denied that his name was Edwards and immediately went in to where his girlfriend was exercising. Shortly thereafter, the two left the gym together."

It was the last known sighting of Laura Liliana Casillas Padilla in Guadalajara.

Later that afternoon, Harlingen got a call at the gym from Stone's old girlfriend. It was the same woman he'd talked to the night before, and she asked about John Edwards again.

"Harlingen said he [Stone] was not there and mentioned he had told Stone/Edwards that she had called," investigators wrote.

The woman erupted at Harlingen over the phone upon learning he'd informed Stone she'd called.

"The woman became furious, threatening that he would be in big trouble for not maintaining the confidentiality of their phone conversation," investigators wrote.

In the days following these events, Harlingen would hear reports of men in dark suits trailing some of his employees and interviewing them at their homes about Stone. He had heard they were agents with the FBI, but they never contacted him.

He didn't think much more about the incident at the time other than to say it was yet another strange episode involving Stone.

When Larry Hanna returned to Las Vegas and learned that a tip had come in from the *Geraldo* show placing Addis at a gym in Guadalajara, he was excited. That excitement turned to anger when he later learned the FBI was not given the time to investigate whether it was, in fact, Addis posing as John Stone at the gym and that Dollie Greenrock Wells had called the gym, prompting Addis to flee.

When it first happened, however, investigators still could not definitively say it was Addis. Only later would investigators confirm through interviews of witnesses that it was, in fact, Addis posing as "John Stone."

Once the FBI was able to interview employees from the gym, Hanna also learned that Addis was now in the company of a young woman from the gym. Hanna later put pen to paper for the FBI on how Addis was able to escape arrest:

"Pursuant to the Rivera program, Albanese's family received information from Rivera's staff of a sighting of Addis being at a Gold's Gym in Guadalajara," Hanna wrote. "The family, not being able to contact me immediately, called the gym and asked for John Addis.

"The FBI attempted to locate Addis by establishing surveillance in the Guadalajara area, but they were unable to locate him. I was ultimately advised by Agent Debbie Calhoun of the Las Vegas office of the FBI that an investigation in the Guadalajara area revealed Addis was positively identified as having lived there recently . . . and that Joann Albanese had not been seen in his company or in the area."

The day John Addis vanished from the gym in Guadalajara was the last time Laura Liliana Casillas Padilla was seen in the city. Her family started to worry when they didn't see her at work or hear from her later that day. That evening, one of her sisters, Jessica Casillas Padilla, went to Laura Liliana's apartment in Guadalajara to check on her.

All of her belongings were there, but she was nowhere to be found. The sister found a note on the floor near a garage at the home. It was from Laura Liliana. It read:

Padres—

Gracias por todo lo que me llamaremos, pero creo que es tiempo de irme. John me propuso matrimonia. Y accepte. Nosotros vamos a estar bien. No se preocupen.
  Por favor, traten de entender, se que tienen razon para molestarse. Recuerden que los quiero mucho. Uds, no hicieron nada mal. Tome una decision. Yo se que estan enojados, pero por favor traten de entender.
  Nosotros uamaremos depues no se preocupen.

Los Quiero Mucho.
Laura Liliana.

Translation:

Parents—Thanks for everything [you] have given me, but I believe that it is time to go [for] me. John proposed marriage to me. I accepted. We are going to be well. Do not worry. [We will] call you. Please, try to understand. . . . I know you may be angry, but please try to understand.

Love Laura Liliana.

None of her belongings were taken from the home. Her Mexican passport and U.S. tourist visa were left behind. The next day, Laura Liliana's panicked father, Miguel

Casillas Rosales, filed a missing-persons report regarding
the disappearance of his daughter. He filed it with the district attorney's office near Parque Alcalde in Guadalajara,
but it does not appear from public records that authorities
there immediately thought Laura Liliana Casillas Padilla
was a victim of foul play.

"Mr. Casillas believes that no murder investigation was
ever initiated as the information indicated that his daughter
was missing, not killed," FBI investigators would later say
in describing their interview with the father of the missing
girl.

Casillas hired a private investigator to search for his
daughter. They traced John Stone's address and found
many of his belongings left behind in his flat. His computer
was not there.

Casillas would never hear from his beautiful daughter
again.

20 ... ABBI

Abbi Silver is one of the most tenacious prosecutorial fighters around, and she's proud of it. She doesn't hesitate to tell people that as a prosecutor in the Clark County, Nevada, district attorney's office in Las Vegas, she earned the nickname "the Iron Maiden bitch" while fighting to defend the rights of women and children in the city for nearly two decades. Part of the nickname, Silver said, came from her toughness on criminals, but the other reason she got the nickname was because she was a woman in a world dominated by white men when she first started as a prosecutor in Southern Nevada, and she had a choice: either be tougher than anyone else or get walked on, and anyone who knows Silver knows that no one steamrolls Abbi.

No one.

"I would completely take [defense attorneys] out in court," Silver said. "I became known as this Iron Maiden bitch of the DA's office, and my reputation was way worse than anyone else's. I had to be tough."

The toughness, however, is really a cover for a very sensitive, kind, extremely funny, colorful, and righteous woman who believes in what she does. Now a Las Vegas justice of the peace, she doles out justice fairly and firmly for both sides. She commits herself to being the fairest judge humanly possible. But when she worked as a prosecutor with the district attorney's office, she was paid to win, and she did just that. She lost only one case in fourteen years as she prosecuted the worst of the worst—rapists, child molesters, and kid killers.

"My first trial ever was a rape trial," Silver said of her start as a prosecutor. "A date rape, and the victim was from the wrong side of the tracks. I took this case into trial after my supervisors were telling me they would have denied charges against the defendant. But I believed her, the jury believed her, and I got [the rapist] three consecutive life sentences. When they said the verdict, guilty, I remember the victim coming up to me, hugging me, sobbing and shaking, and saying, 'Thank you!' That's what changed me. I was like, wow, I can help people."

Silver is as beautiful as a Nevada sunset. She has long brown hair, a glowing face, and a fireball personality. She has a celebrity crush on rock star Bret Michaels, of the glam-rock band Poison. She will speak her mind in every instance and not really care what the ramifications are. The truth is the truth with Silver, and as a prosecutor, she was a reporter's dream because she talked and talked and talked about her cases with a passion, never asking to go off the record, and not really worrying about speaking about her case in public because the truth is the truth.

Silver was born and raised in a family of five children. Her dad is a doctor, her mom a housewife. The Silver children had an idyllic life growing up in the shadows of Hoover Dam in Boulder City. Boulder City is situated twenty-three miles from Las Vegas, and it is one of the most charming communities in Nevada. It is a refuge from the hustle of Sin City, and it is a community that still values and protects its small-town feel despite constant threats of encroachment and development from a steady flow of Vegas refugees who are looking to get out of the Vegas rat race by venturing out to Boulder City. The city of fifteen thousand people was born out of the construction of the dam, commonly referred to in Vegas as the "Eighth Wonder of the World."

"When I was growing up in Boulder City, it was a great life," she said. "There were maybe five thousand people there at the time. In the early 1970s, we would have to drive all the way to Las Vegas just to go shopping. There was no fast food; [there was] a Frosty Freeze so you could get burritos, and that was about it. Now they have a Taco Bell. Where was the Taco Bell when I was there? We had nowhere to eat! I would have loved a Taco Bell.

"I rode my bike everywhere, even to school, and my dog, Heidi, would follow me," Silver said. "She would sit there next to my bike while I was in school, and I would look out the window and see my dog sitting next to my bike, waiting for me to get out of school. When I got done, my dog, Heidi, would literally be there waiting for me. My dad loved the West, and he wanted us to grow up out here in the mountains. We lived on the fifth hole of the golf course, and every night [my dog and I] would be out in the sprinklers and sand pits. A great childhood."

Silver got much of her competitive nature from sports. She played varsity tennis her freshman year, she swam on the varsity swim team, and she played volleyball and softball. She always wanted to be a cheerleader and was not accepted onto the cheerleading team for five straight years. She persisted and made it onto the senior cheerleading team after the family relocated to Las Vegas.

"When I didn't want to play in band because the outfits were ugly, I became a majorette," Silver said. "Then it was cheerleading."

The cheerleading led to a great gig as a cheerleader for the NBA's Utah Jazz for two years when the team moved west.

"I was really good at it in my day," Silver said. "I made cheerleader my senior year, then went pro the next. I was very driven. Very driven. Nothing came easy to me. I had to practice and practice and practice. It was really cool being an NBA cheerleader. I've got pictures of me with Kareem Abdul-Jabbar and Magic Johnson. Now, when I tell anyone who's into sports, they are like, wow! That's really cool. Well, hey, I just liked to cheer and throw my pom-poms."

Silver dreamed of being a professional dancer, but her father advised against it, urging her to be a doctor or lawyer. Knee surgery derailed the dream anyway, and after graduating from the University of Nevada at Las Vegas, she went to law school in Los Angeles.

"[My best friend and I] were twenty-one, and the average age of everyone in law school was like thirty-three, and remember, I was a cheerleader, so I had the biggest hair," Silver said. "Everybody just looked at us and laughed and figured we were going to fail out."

She graduated with honors and thought she was going to "go into corporate law to make money." But after taking a job as a judicial law clerk for a Las Vegas judge, she was recommended for a position at the Clark County District Attorney's Office, and she never looked back. She rose through the district attorney's office by being tough in a world where, at the time at least, women faced some very serious obstacles in becoming a top prosecutor.

"I was one of only five women when I started, and they asked me [during the job interview], 'Are you going to have kids?'" Silver recalled. "As a woman prosecutor I guess you aren't supposed to. They didn't want any maternity leave. Then the word I heard from my fellow district attorneys after I got hired was that they just hired a cheerleader. What the hell? Then it was, I'm having an affair . . . and I was married at the time to a cop for twelve years. It's just because I was young and female. I wish I had as much action as they were claiming, but it was hard on me. It really was. I don't like to throw the woman card down, but I'm telling you, it was twice as hard for me. When I'd show up in court, I'd get asked if I was taking everything down. They thought I was a court reporter. One attorney . . . said to me on the record, in front of a whole courtroom, during argument, 'I don't know what's wrong with her. It must be a bad time of the month for her.' On the record. It was a lot harder for females. It was not easy."

Over time, Silver became frustrated with her inability to get major trial experience. Finally, she confronted a supervisor, who responded, "What, are you accusing me of sexual discrimination?"

Enraged, Silver chewed his ass out, and it apparently impressed the veteran prosecutor. The next day she was reassigned to trial duty. She spent much of the next two decades prosecuting rapists and child abusers. It was noble work. After years of doing it, she requested a transfer and was assigned to screen cases to determine whether charges were warranted against a suspect.

This was when she heard of John Patrick Addis for the very first time.

Las Vegas police detective Larry Hanna had spent two years searching for John Patrick Addis but didn't have a warrant. If Addis was located as a suspect wanted for questioning in a disappearance, it was very possible that Addis could just walk away. Addis was a cop and knew the rules—Hanna thought it was probable this scenario might very well play out if he ever found Addis. Hanna was convinced Joann was dead, but he knew getting a warrant for murder would be a tough sell. He nonetheless prepared a comprehensive warrant application for the Clark County District Attorney's Office and summarized how he believed Joann was murdered in her home.

Based on the above information and the circumstances surrounding Joann Albanese's disappearance, it is the investigator's belief that during the evening of 8/19/95, or early morning of 8/20/95, John Addis, a skilled police officer with a background in homicide investigations, a special weapons and tactical officer, and survivalist; and Joann Albanese, known to have a volatile personality and temper by both family and LVMPD investigators from an incident [at juvenile hall], became involved in an argument over the termination of their relationship, which Addis historically relied upon to maintain his lifestyle. Or, Albanese discovered that Addis was living under an assumed identity; or Albanese learned that Addis was planning to extort money from her in some fashion. During the course of this argument, which occurred soon after Albanese stepped from the shower, as evidence[d] by her bathrobe lying on the floor, no clothing missing, and the jewelry she removed only to shower remaining in the bathroom, Addis killed Albanese by either strangulation, breaking her neck, or damaging a vital internal organ sufficient to cause death without external trauma—this assumption due to the lack of obvious physical trauma at the scene.

After killing Albanese, Addis placed her body in her vehicle; spot cleaned the residence in an effort to eliminate any evidence of his true identity; drove her body into the desert and disposed of it somewhere between Las Vegas and Prescott, where it may never be discovered, and ultimately concealed her vehicle in Little Hell's Canyon. Addis, concerned that the family may be aware of her disappearance and fearful of an encounter with law enforcement, abandoned his personal property and fled to Mexico to avoid detection and prosecution for the murder of Joann Albanese.

Based on the above information, an affidavit for a warrant on the charge of murder against Addis will be presented to the Clark County District Attorney's Office. Subsequent to the issuance of a warrant for Addis' arrest on the charge of murder, investigators will seek an unlawful flight to avoid prosecution warrant from the Federal Bureau of Investigation to obtain

their assistance in relocating Addis and retrieving him
from Mexico should he still be located in that country.

Hanna walked over to the district attorney's office on
Third Street in downtown Las Vegas with his massive
case file in search of a prosecutor who would listen. He
knew ahead of time it was going to be tough meeting the
burden of a murder warrant. He had a very circumstantial
case, because Joann's body hadn't been found and there
was hardly any physical evidence. However, with the abuse
allegations against Addis by his prior wives, his flight from
Las Vegas, and the witness testimony of his abusive relationship with Joann as well as the information from Joann's
mother that Joann had been planning to break off the relationship, Hanna felt a murder warrant for Addis was justi-
fied, and he found his champion in Abbi Silver.

"Hanna walked in, he was with missing persons, he brings
me this file, and said, 'I want you to look at this case,'" Silver recalled. "I was really into the domestic-violence laws . . .
and the case seemed very, very interesting."

"Hanna told me, 'He killed her. There's no doubt. You
need to read all this, go through it, and make your determination. We still haven't found her body.'"

Silver read the entire case file and was fascinated. A
former Alaska state trooper forced his first wife, Emma,
to live in a home with no running water in Alaska, then
kidnapped their kids and flew them to Montana for eight
months without letting Emma know where they were.

"An abusive, controlling kook," Silver said. "No running water in Alaska? He's like a wilderness man who
gets dropped off in the wilderness to hunt caribou; then

he kidnaps the kids. . . . It's so weird . . . one of the craziest stories ever."

"Him being a homicide investigator, knowing all the ins and outs, who better to hinder an investigation by making a body disappear with no physical evidence? . . . I mean, who would be better at it than him?" Silver said. "We speculated she tried to break up, it didn't work, he strangled her, killed her, put her body in the back of the car, and took her to Arizona. Now he's in Mexico. The guy's incredible.

"We thought Canada or Mexico—Canada could have worked as well because he liked the cold country," Silver said. "To me, Canada seemed more natural. Then we had heard there had been sightings of him in Mexico, and every step of the way, it's too late. He's gone. What a weird, mysterious character."

Silver reinterviewed all the witnesses and was very impressed with Tom Albanese, who, under difficult circumstances, did everything he could to help Silver's inquiry while at the same time trying to raise two daughters who still yearned for their mother.

"A really nice man," Silver said. "Very helpful even though they had gone through a pretty bad divorce."

Silver, like Hanna, immediately heard stories about Joann's fiery temper. A secretary who saw the case file and the name Joann Albanese immediately recognized the name from the incident in which Joann's daughter had a minor encounter with Las Vegas police juvenile detectives. The secretary, who was working in juvenile at the time, recounted how Joann Albanese had torn into the Juvenile Detective Division and read the riot act to anyone in front of her.

"What a bitch!" the secretary said as she recalled the incident at juvenile hall for Silver.

Silver, though, could identify with such cursory judgments. She recognized that Joann was a tough woman who was single and trying to raise two daughters. She came to admire her as she learned more and more about her. She was tough, just like Silver.

"I heard she was super feisty, but I'm sure she's like everyone else: someone with many different sides to her," Silver said. "Joann was a very together woman, very pretty. Maybe they called her a bitch because she knew what she wanted and stood up for herself.

"I'm kinda likin' her, but that's me," Silver said. "I don't see a problem with being assertive."

The more she learned about Joann, the more she thought that she had definitely been murdered and discarded in the desert somewhere. Everything about Joann was organized. She was highly respected at work, "a very sharp lady" who put her children first in everything she did. There was no way in hell Joann would just take off and leave the kids, her purse, her jewelry, and her money behind to run off with Addis.

"She was a very attractive woman in her midthirties, divorced, and having been there myself, I know it's really hard to find a nice guy out there," Silver said. "You ain't young anymore. You become much more refined in your tastes. She liked nice things, and there's nothing wrong with that. A very pretty gal, and she wanted something more. When she dated, she dated more attractive men. I learned she was a very loving mom and loved those two girls. That was the number-one reason why I felt she was murdered. A mother who fights for custody and loves the children . . . if she can get hooked up with a guy, great, but she would never leave these two girls for a man. She was a mom first.

"I really looked at more of the circumstances," Silver said. "There really wasn't anything physical as far as evidence. There [were] some missing pillows; she left her money, her wallet, her jewelry. Who would do that? Who would just grab a pillow and go? Not just Joann . . . no one would do that to go to Hells Canyon for a camping trip.

"If you really sit and dissect who she is and her personality, she's someone I admire," Silver said. "I'm a female who had been in her situation, divorced . . . [and] besides John Patrick Addis, she was doing very well for herself. She had every right to be out in the world, dating, and she liked attractive men. John was attractive."

The prosecutor was very impressed with the investigation Hanna had put together: "A great job," she said. "No one would have worked up a missing-persons case like he did and taken it as seriously as he did."

But three years had passed, and the three-year state statute for kidnapping was running out. If she didn't get an indictment by August 1998, she would never be able to charge Addis with kidnapping, and there was no guarantee she'd get a murder warrant. She felt she, at a minimum, had a good chance at a warrant if she took the case for an indictment in front of a grand jury. She reinterviewed all the witnesses and found Joann's friend, Tara Rivera, to be a very valuable witness who offered disturbing information about Addis's sexual obsessiveness and his demonstrated attempts to control everything about Joann's life.

"Tara knew her the best," Silver said.

Silver focused much of her attention on Addis's three

ex-wives to determine how extensive the abuse was in the marriages. She knew about the kidnapping of the children in Alaska, but she figured the ex-wives had much more to tell about abuse. She vetted those issues with the ex-wives, but according to Silver, they were reluctant to testify. They were all terrified of Addis and what he might do if he knew they'd testified against him in front of a grand jury.

"[With Joann], he left his penis inside of her, watched her pee, and because of my experience and background, I recognized not only is he controlling and, we thought, abusive physically but I also didn't think it was his first rodeo," Silver said. "The fact he'd been married before, he's done something to them, too.

"I'm the one who found the ex-wives," Silver said. "What those ex-wives had to say was remarkable. We knew he was a trooper, lived like a weirdo, all that kind of stuff, but I don't think Hanna knew the extent of the abuse directed at the ex-wives. I had to compel them to come. I'll throw you in jail or you are coming to the grand jury. They were terrified."

Silver felt the testimony of Joann's mother, Margarete Greenrock, was critical. Greenrock said the night Joann disappeared she told her she was going to break off her relationship with Addis.

"She gave us motive," the prosecutor said.

Silver approached her bosses for permission to take the case to the grand jury, and she ran into resistance almost immediately. No body, no crime. At best, there were suspicions but likely not enough to get an indictment.

"I was convinced and felt it was a strong case, and they laughed about it," Silver said. "Some of them were convinced she was on an island, drinking a piña colada and calling it a day. I said, 'Maybe you would do that, but most people don't just get up and leave, go to an island, and drink a piña colada without telling other people, including their small children.'"

Undeterred, Silver decided to ignore her bosses and take it to the grand jury. She felt it was her duty to do so, and she would worry about any potential repercussions later.

"There was no body, so I knew it was going to be a difficult case," she said.

On June 25, 1998, Silver kicked off the effort to indict John Patrick Addis on a murder charge.

"Good morning, ladies and gentlemen of the grand jury," she said. "Today you are here on the case of state of Nevada versus John Patrick Addis, aka John Edwards, the defendant listed in the proposed indictment. It is charged in the indictment, the defendant, with two crimes: one, murder, open murder, that on or about August 19, 1995, and August 20, 1995, the defendant, John Patrick Addis, did then and there willfully, feloniously, without authority of law, and with premeditation and deliberation, and with malice aforethought, kill Joann Albanese, a human being, by manner and means unknown.

"Count two, first-degree kidnapping," Silver said. "Did willfully, unlawfully, feloniously, and without authority of law, seize [and] kidnap or carry away Joann Albanese, a human being, with the intent to hold or detain the said Joann Albanese against her will and without her consent, for the purpose of killing the person or inflicting substantial bodily harm upon this said Joann Albanese.

"Ladies and gentlemen, those two crimes, murder and

first-degree kidnapping, the elements of those offenses, are contained within the indictment itself. You also have before you statute books regarding the law on both murder and first-degree kidnapping."

Silver's first witness was Amber Albanese. The teen recounted the panic she felt when she returned home on the night of August 20, 1995, and found an empty home with her mother's purse and jewelry left behind.

"It was very unusual that her belongings were there, because she takes her purse with her," Amber said. "It's got her money, her driver's license, everything. I believe her keys were even there. . . . Even if she's going across the street, she brings it with her."

The next witness was Thomas Albanese, who said Joann would never leave the children home alone without calling him first. He also recounted how unusual it was to find the bedroom door of the home open when Joann wasn't home.

"She would always take her purse," Tom Albanese said. "She always wore her watch, as well as her bracelet and the ring she had. [The bed] was not made, and I noticed that the comforter was off to the side. . . . Very unusual. Joann would always make up the bed before she left for the day unless she was in a rush to get out of there. That was very unusual to see the bed in that condition."

Joann's sister recalled how unusual it was for Joann to just be absent from her home when the kids were there. She recalled searching through Addis's truck, finding the license plates and envelope with the name John Addis on it.

"He talked about a place called Little Hells Canyon, and I said it sounds like an awful place," Wells said. "He said, 'Actually, it's a really beautiful place,' and he thought that he might be going there soon.

"He had asked me what was the largest game I'd ever hunted," Wells recalled. "I said small things like quail, deer, you know, things like that. And he said he didn't mean small in size. He meant small in intelligence. And I looked at him, and I just said . . . that a human was the only thing intelligent and no, I've never hunted human. He looked at me and said, 'I would.'"

Tara Rivera talked of how she had introduced Addis to Joann, and how Addis, over time, became completely obsessed with Joann. He wanted to control everything in her life. He wanted her to have sex constantly and walk around the house naked. She also recounted the bizarre encounter she'd had with Addis on that dinner outing, when he had become incensed by a routine comment. His personality seemed to change right before her eyes.

"He just snapped, Jekyll and Hyde. He just came out and said, 'I'm the best. I told you that I owe you my life for what you did. You introduced me to Joann,'" Rivera recalled.

"And he got louder, and people were looking and staring, and I got very uncomfortable at that time, and my husband grabbed my left arm, [and] I immediately said to my husband, 'It's time to leave.' I observed an outrage, like his eyes were bulging. He looked deranged."

Rivera told the grand jury of getting goose bumps over the eerie incident and of telling Joann the next day that she needed to dump Addis because "there's something wrong."

Glenn Wilcox Jr. recounted for the grand jury how Addis had asked him to cover his shift at the 24-Hour Fitness, then vanished.

"He parked [his truck] on the side of the house and

backed it in so that you couldn't see a license plate," Wilcox said. "I just thought that was peculiar. [After Joann disappeared], I went in his room to see if he was there, and that's when I noticed that all of his things were packed up where they weren't before. His computer was packed up, and he was always working on his computer. He was writing. The computer was boxed up. All his belongings were boxed up as much as possible."

Detective Larry Hanna outlined the entire investigation for the grand jury, saying he was convinced Joann was dead.

"What we began learning on the twenty-second of August is that we weren't sure who we were dealing with," Hanna said. "We may have a problem."

Detective Gordon Diffendaffer, of the Yavapai County Sheriff's Office, recounted finding the vehicle and conducting a massive, prolonged search for Joann's body:

"I made contact with our sheriff's office dive team, and they searched the lake for bodies. We found none."

Jim McCann flew down from Alaska to recount for the grand jury Addis's background in law enforcement and crime-scene investigations, and he told how Addis had abruptly disappeared and quit the police force. The Alaska homicide detective also gave the grand jury some background on Addis, saying he was a very skilled outdoorsman who could survive off the land.

"Well, he would do just the general moose hunting, like most people would do, get twelve-hundred pounds of meat for his family for the season," McCann said. "But I remember one trip he took in particular that was a little bit beyond what most of any of the rest of us would do, which is when it gets cold, we go to Las Vegas. When it gets very cold,

John went hunting. He flew out to hunt caribou out into the wilderness. He was dropped off, and it was 40 or 50 below. [Dropped off] by airplane."

Addis's first wife, Emma, recounted the abuse and kidnapping of her four children. Addis's second wife, Sarah Rayder, talked of the moment when she realized something was very wrong with her new husband: he revealed to her a bizarre plot for kidnapping his children from his first marriage.

"He would be posing as a woman," she said. "He would dress as a woman, shave his legs, and take on the appearance of a woman. He would take the children. Possibly to Australia or Canada."

The suspect's third wife, Toni Martinez, told of violent domestic abuse at the hands of Addis. And, finally, Joann's mother offered tearful testimony about losing her beloved daughter.

"She was a good daughter, excellent daughter," Margarete Greenrock said. "She didn't drink. She didn't smoke. Two or three times a day I talked to her. Sometimes four times a day on the phone. I would say out of seven days, six days. . . . We were very attached to each other.

"They made a reservation for dinner in the Hilton, and [my daughter said], 'I want to tell him that I'm not ready to be married,'" Greenrock said. "I said, 'Be careful. You've got to know what you're doing.'"

"Have you ever heard from her again after this?" Silver asked.

"No," Greenrock said through tears.

With no body and little physical evidence, Silver received a grand jury indictment for John Patrick Addis on murder and kidnapping charges in August of 1998. The prosecutor was ecstatic. She knew she'd finally made a stand for Joann—a woman who had been brutally victimized and taken away from her two daughters with extreme cruelty.

"It was amazing to get this indictment," Silver said. "I was on top of the world, and I went into my boss's office singing, 'Nah ne nah ne nah ne!' It was landmark in Nevada to get an indictment for murder without a body. A pretty big deal."

Detective Hanna felt a great sense of relief. He thought the warrant would help him one day catch Addis, and he had high praise for Silver's efforts. But what happened next totally surprised him. Just a month later, in October, he got a call from the Yavapai County Sheriff's Office.

A hunter had stumbled upon some bones in the mountains near where Joann's car had been found. The detective would later confirm, through DNA testing, that the bones were, in fact, Joann's. Remarkably, the remains had apparently been hauled up a mountain and dumped in a discreet location. No one had ever thought to go up the mountain to look for the body in the search. It seemed like a very unlikely place to put a body.

"It was a huge mountain," Hanna said. "You don't carry dead bodies up a mountain. He killed her up here in Vegas, then drove this treacherous route, carrying her up the mountain, and put her there. They didn't search upward, which is logical. People don't carry bodies up a mountain, but . . . [Addis] did."

The remains were just bones, so an autopsy could not discern a cause of death. However, the fact that Joann's remains were found in a remote location where her car was discarded only reaffirmed for homicide investigators that her death was clearly a murder.

"Remains found in the Arizona desert last week were confirmed on Friday as belonging to Joann Albanese, a Las Vegas mother missing for nearly three years," wrote the *Las Vegas Review-Journal* newspaper on October 20, 1998. "The man charged in her death, former Alaska state trooper John Addis, is still nowhere to be found."

21 . . . MANHUNT

With the warrant in hand, the investigation and search for John Patrick Addis seemed like it would get some new life. Hanna issued a wanted flyer and distributed it again throughout the United States. With no way to trace Addis's whereabouts, generating publicity and reaching out to other law enforcement agencies seemed like the most likely ways to get new information. The wanted poster pictured Addis wearing a moustache and smiling. It read:

WANTED: MURDER/KIDNAP

John Patrick Addis

On August 19, 1995, Joann Albanese (remains found) disappeared from her residence in Las Vegas, along with her boyfriend John Edwards. Investigation revealed Edwards's true identity to be John Patrick

Addis, an ex-police investigator, who was a certified instructor in crime scene and death investigations; a skilled marksman, survivalist and pilot; and found to be adept at manufacturing false identification. Our investigation has established a history of Addis meeting women at health clubs, where he would be a member or employee; aligning himself with a woman; moving in with her; and eventually leaving abruptly, often defrauding the woman of money. Our investigation has traced Addis through numerous states throughout the United States. However, there has been no indication of additional women he has been associated with as missing or deceased. Our investigation has culminated in the issuance of a warrant for Addis' arrest for kidnapping and murder of Joann H. Albanese. Anyone with information regarding Addis' whereabouts are asked to contact the Las Vegas Metropolitan Police Department, Federal Bureau of Investigation or your local police department.

Hanna got the federal government to put Addis on an Interpol alert that would be distributed throughout the world. The notice alerted police agencies to the following, with the header of "Fugitive Wanted for Prosecution." A mug shot on the notice showed Addis photographed in 1995 on his gym card. His fingerprints were displayed in charts from Juneau, Alaska, state police records.

Interpol Red—
Warning: This person may be armed, violent and dangerous.
Present Family Name: Addis.

Date and Place of Birth: 19th, September, 1950—
Flint, Michigan, United States.

Nationality: Citizen of the United States.

Identity Documents: United States passport, United
States Social Security Card [two numbers given].

Also known as: Edwards, John H. [a real person's
name]. Elliot, John.

Description: Height 185 cm, weight 90 kg, light
brown hair, blue or green eyes.

Occupation: Health and fitness club employee. Former police officer [Alaska state trooper], homicide detective, instructor in crime scene analysis,
skilled marksman, pilot, outdoor survivalist.

Language spoken: English.

Regions/countries likely to be visited: Australia,
Canada, Central and South America, Mexico,
United Kingdom.

Judicial information/summary: In August 1995,
Addis was living with a woman in Las Vegas,
Nevada. On 19th August 1995, Addis and the
woman disappeared. Woman's purse and other
items were found in her bedroom. On 10th October 1998, the fragmented, skeletal remains of
her body were found in a remote area outside
Prescott, Arizona. Death was a result of strangulation or a broken neck.

Charges: Murder, kidnapping [first degree], unlawful flight to avoid prosecution.

Action to be taken if traced: Immediately inform
Interpol Washington, and the ICPO Interpol Gen-
eral Secretariat that the fugitive has been found.
For countries which consider red notices to be

> valid requests for provisional arrest, please
> provisionally arrest the fugitive. Extradition will
> be requested from any country with which the
> requesting country is linked by a bilateral extra-
> dition treaty, an extradition convention or by any
> other convention or treaty containing provisions
> on extradition.

"I gave the media and law enforcement everything," Hanna said. "Getting the feds involved was really impor- tant, because once you have the warrant, you can get an unlawful flight to avoid prosecution warrant, and you can get the feds involved anywhere. Now I've got federal assistance. I have the out-of-country stuff, but the warrant helps, because anywhere in the world, they could feasi- bly pick him up. Then I put him in Interpol. Missing and wanted for murder. Next, he made the FBI's Top 10 most wanted in America."

After the warrant was issued, the national television show *America's Most Wanted* picked up the story of John Patrick Addis with a vengeance. The show's founder, John Walsh, seemed to take a personal interest in the case, as the warrant allowed the show to begin airing segments. Generally, the show does not air pieces on cases without a warrant issued. Walsh then appeared on *Larry King Live* and on CNN and pleaded for tipsters to come forward with information on Addis's whereabouts. The segment started with a video introduction about Addis with a Walsh voice-over:

WALSH: "Twenty years ago, John Patrick Addis was a cop's cop. He was a young, ambitious state trooper in Fairbanks, Alaska. He quickly advanced from patrolling the highways to the criminal investigation division. Addis started dating Joann Albanese, a successful businesswoman and divorced mother of two. On August 19, 1995, Joann decided to tell Addis that the relationship was over. Four days later, Joann's car was found abandoned two hundred miles away near Prescott, Arizona. There was no sign of Joann or John Addis. Investigators were certain Addis had murdered Joann Albanese, but he left no physical evidence, no defined crime scene, and most important, no corpse."

Walsh described Addis as a "tough guy to catch," and King asked whether the murder of Albanese was a "crime of passion."

"Well, he was an exploiter of women," Walsh said. "When he stopped being a cop, he became a body builder and worked in gyms, went to Las Vegas. He exploited several women. He was a hustler."

America's Most Wanted aired shows on Addis a remarkable eight times from November 21, 1998, to May 28, 2005. They also produced a comprehensive package about Addis on the Internet:

John Patrick Addis was an intriguing individual. In the 1980s, Addis was a state trooper in Alaska. He rose quickly from patrolling the highways of the Alaskan interior to homicide detective.

By 1995, Addis had relocated to Las Vegas, and reinvented himself as a body-builder and personal trainer. While working at a local gym, Addis met an attractive divorcee named Joann Albanese. . . . On August 19, 1995, Joann Albanese disappeared. So did John Addis.

But in mid-1998, a hunter stumbled across human skeletal remains in the Arizona desert. DNA tests proved it was Joann Albanese.

Investigators have since learned that in 1997, Addis was living in Guadalajara, Mexico, under the aliases John Charles Edwards and John Charles Stone. There, he began dating a Mexican woman named Laura Liliana Padilla, who was twenty-six at the time.

But Addis and Laura Liliana vanished from Guadalajara and have not been seen since.

Nancy Grace, the former Atlanta prosecutor turned television true-crime maven, ran segments twice on her show as well.

Hanna said the multiple television shows and media interest, particularly from *America's Most Wanted*, generated hundreds and hundreds of leads. Each one of the leads was followed up on.

"We are all thinking, he went to Mexico, he went to Mexico," the detective said. "But we are still putting it out there, and we got leads. Tons of them. Like I'm saying, five hundred leads, every state in the union, coast to coast, he was supposedly seen in. We have to go and try to verify. What was the sighting, and was it him or not? I had packets all put together. Send them out. Here's his prints, here's his photos, and you send out to the local agencies. You find this individual and see if it is him. It never panned out.

"Hundreds," Hanna said of the number of leads. "Over the years I'm sure we had five hundred leads. Depending on how good the lead was, we'd send all that stuff out. Developed a form letter. First started faxing it, then e-mailing it, it changed as time went on. Not a one panned out."

From the day John Patrick Addis was last seen in the Guadalajara gym, he had simply vanished. Hanna had obtained an investigator's dream for media coverage of his missing-persons case, but not one of hundreds of leads panned out.

Addis had vanished like a ghost in the night.

He was untraceable, and it would take eight more years to find him.

22 . . . MY DAUGHTER IS MISSING

Miguel Casillas Rosales, his wife, sons, and daughter were completely heartbroken over the disappearance of Laura Liliana Casillas Padilla in the months and years after she disappeared from Gold's Gym in Guadalajara. It was a truly devastating event for the family. Laura Liliana was extremely close to her family. They worked together. They talked on the phone regularly. Laura Liliana was in continual contact with her father as well, and the note telling her loved ones that she was running off to marry John Stone was a terribly traumatic event. Casillas, deep in his heart, knew something was wrong because Laura Liliana never returned to collect her belongings or her money from her bank accounts. The bank accounts were never accessed again by his daughter.

Casillas would, like Dollie Greenrock Wells, embark on a years-long search for his daughter. He walked the streets of Guadalajara constantly, hoping he would by chance find her or stumble across Stone. He went to the local authorities, but they treated the case as a missing person—not a homicide—and issued a missing-persons release. There wasn't, however, the massive police search like the one carried out in Las Vegas by police detective Larry Hanna in the search for Joann Albanese. Frustrated, Casillas hired a private detective who tracked down Alberto Abreau and located the flat Stone had been staying in for free in Guadalajara. Stone's belongings had been left behind, but there were no clues to indicate where the couple had gone. The private investigator never was able to collect any clues that might potentially provide a pathway to Laura Liliana's whereabouts. For two years, the Casillas family was left to grieve and wonder what had happened to their beautiful and promising daughter.

However, in approximately 1999—two years after Laura Liliana's disappearance—Casillas received some startling information. He learned from a friend, Salvador Magdaleno, that John Charles Stone may not have been the true name of the American his daughter had been dating. Casillas learned secondhand through Magdaleno that a manager at Gold's Gym, Stevie Harlingen, had had a bizarre phone call the evening before Stone disappeared from an American woman claiming she knew the man known as "John Stone" but that his real name was John Edwards. Shortly after hearing of this phone call, Stone and Laura Liliana disappeared.

There is a slight discrepancy in the public record regarding the day Stone fled from the gym. Harlingen's recollection was that Stone, upon hearing the name "John Edwards," had rushed to another part of the Guadalajara fitness center, tracked down Laura Liliana—who was in the gym—and fled. Casillas, however, told the FBI he believes Laura Liliana was not in the gym at the time, and that Stone rushed to Laura Liliana's home in Guadalajara, possibly to kidnap her.

"Mr. Casillas believes that Stone went to the Casillas residence that same afternoon and left with his daughter," the FBI reported. "It is his understanding Stone went to pick her up at approximately the hour of the midday meal. No one else was home when he arrived at the residence. Casillas was also told police officials later went to Gold's Gym looking for Stone, who had already left."

A wave of panic swept through Casillas upon learning Stone was not who he said he was. It was the same panic the loved ones of Joann Albanese felt when they learned that John Edwards was really John Patrick Addis.

Casillas tracked down Harlingen at Gold's Gym, and according to Casillas, Harlingen "refused to provide much useful information." Harlingen, however, showed Casillas another residence in Guadalajara where Stone had stayed.

"None of Casillas's daughter's friends had any knowledge of plans for her to run away with Stone," the FBI reported. "Mr. Casillas said that someone later commented that his daughter had discussed going to Vancouver, British Columbia, with Stone, but no details were given. Laura [Liliana] left behind her passport and all her other belongings when she disappeared."

Casillas told the FBI his daughter worked for him and was very bright. Law enforcement, summarizing his comments about his daughter in police reports, indicated Casillas "felt that, if she had been taken by force, she would be smart enough to figure out a way to escape and return home."

"Laura [Liliana] had no reason to run away," the FBI reported. "[Casillas] and his wife enjoyed an excellent relationship with their daughter.... He cannot explain why his daughter apparently wrote a note saying that she was leaving, but then took nothing with her. He indicated that it may have been that she planned to leave with Stone, wrote the note, but then departed with him with the expectation of returning to get her things. Casillas said the bank statements for his daughter still arrive at their home. The money in her account has not been removed and no transactions have occurred since her departure. He feels certain that, had she left to marry Stone, she would have, at some point, withdrawn funds from her account."

Harlingen, meanwhile, recounted the shock of learning two years later from Magdaleno that Laura Liliana had never returned home after disappearing from the gym that day in 1997.

"Magdaleno explained that the girl disappeared, apparently that same day, and was never heard from again," the FBI wrote in reports. "Harlingen felt terrible, and told Magdaleno he would speak to the girl's father if it would be helpful."

A meeting was arranged, and Harlingen met Casillas. He learned from the missing girl's father that the young woman "simply vanished, not taking her money, nor any other belongings." Laura Liliana, as an employee of her father's, also had access to substantial amounts of cash from the family business but never accessed any of that money, either.

Harlingen felt terrible about the incident, but he hoped the matter would eventually resolve itself and Laura Liliana would one day return home.

Three more painful years passed for the Casillas family with no word from their daughter. Harlingen heard nothing more until November 2002, when an incident occurred that rocked him to the core. He was in the U.S. Consulate Office in Guadalajara to secure some paperwork when he noticed a law enforcement wanted poster on a wall. He took a close look at the wanted poster and immediately recognized the man pictured in the document as the man he knew as "John Stone." The wanted poster was, however, for John Patrick Addis, who was being sought for a murder in Las Vegas. Harlingen quickly concluded the man he'd known as "John Stone" was actually an American named John Patrick Addis, and he was devastated.

"He spoke to someone in the consulate regarding this matter and got a copy of the flyer, which he took home to show his wife," the FBI reported. "When he realized that Stone was wanted for murder in the United States, and that he had left with the girl from the gym who was never seen again, Harlingen became very upset. He was angry with Stone and felt sorry he had not been able to prevent the tragedy."

Harlingen became very angry over the fact that the caller in 1997 had not just told him the truth—that she was calling for John Patrick Addis, who was wanted for murder. If he had known the truth, he would have never mentioned the call to Stone and would have instead contacted the authorities immediately.

"He pointed out he was not a close friend of Stone's and never would have protected him," the FBI wrote in a report summarizing their interview with Harlingen. "Had the unknown female caller mentioned that Stone was wanted in the States, [Harlingen] would have been happy to cooperate in Stone's apprehension by law enforcement officials. After seeing the flyer in the Consulate, Harlingen gave a copy to Chava Magdaleno, requesting that he make it available to the father of the missing girl. Harlingen said that he did not have the heart to speak to the father himself."

Casillas was devastated upon learning "John Stone" was actually a John Patrick Addis wanted for murder in the United States. He immediately feared the worst. He hadn't heard from his daughter in nearly six years. He rushed to the U.S. Consulate in Guadalajara to gather as much information as possible. An American investigator produced a series of photos of Addis provided to them by Las Vegas police, and Casillas identified "John Stone" as the man wanted in America under his real name, "John Addis."

"[This agent] was able to observe that the man in the photos did, in fact, appear to be identical to photos of John Patrick Addis," an FBI agent wrote.

Officials at the U.S. Consulate's Office notified Las Vegas police detective Larry Hanna in an e-mail. Hanna knew Addis had disappeared from Guadalajara in 1997, but he had been unaware that a woman was missing, too. An officer with diplomatic security at the Consulate wrote to the detective:

"The missing girl's name is Laura Liliana Casillas Padilla. Her father, Miguel Casillas Rosales, says she's been missing now for about five years, and that she disappeared the same time Addis did. The contact . . . said Addis was last seen at Gold's Gym around two to three years ago. I'm not sure who's right about the time frame, but I'd think the father would have a much greater interest in this matter; thus I'd defer to his estimate of five years."

Hanna, in shock, responded via e-mail, urging an immediate inquiry:

"I hope you received my e-mail with the background letter and flyer on the Addis/Stone investigation. As well, I hope you've got the attention at the FBI. If you should hear anything on what the FBI or local police may do with this, please let me know. I would like to speak with whomever is handling this . . . but getting in touch may be problematic. Thanks again for the information you gave me. And, did I mention, Addis is listed and wanted with Interpol? I got him listed as a fugitive a couple of years ago with a promise to drag him back from anywhere he's located."

The heartbreak for Casillas, meanwhile, was overwhelming. He presumed his daughter could very well be dead and that he might never learn what happened to her. It would take three more years to learn the fate of his beloved Laura Liliana.

23 ... PURE EVIL

John Patrick Addis and his new wife, Laura Liliana Casillas Padilla, showed up in Tuxtla Gutiérrez, Chiapas, Mexico, sometime in 1997. The couple had fled Guadalajara without even getting the money out of Laura Liliana's bank account, presumably because Addis didn't want to hang around a second longer than he had to, given that an American had called the gym looking for him. The two relocated to Chiapas, the most southern state in Mexico, which is bordered by the Pacific to the south and Guatemala to the east. It is a well-known tourist stop because of its incredible natural beauty. Chiapas offers a stunning natural landscape featuring everything from volcanoes and mountain ranges to intensely beautiful waterfalls and cloud forests that spread across much of the state. The area receives a significant amount of rainfall every year; the average temperature is 68 degrees, and two rivers in Chiapas, the Usumacinta and Grijalva, are the most glorious rivers in all of Mexico. The state is home to great history and culture featuring Mayan descendants and the ancient Mayan cities of Bonampak and Palenque. Chiapas also has one of the most rural populations in the country, and it is the place where the Zapatista National Liberation Army formed. The capital city the couple settled in, Tuxtla Gutiérrez, is home to roughly 3.6 million people. It is a truly charming city featuring incredible architecture and history, including Palenque, which offers tourists the chance to walk stone stairwells and towers crafted by the Mayans thousands of years ago. Tuxtla Gutiérrez is also a city big enough for the couple to slide into without a great deal of attention or notice.

Little is known about the couple's life in Chiapas over the next nine years. It is known that Addis, now posing as "J. Charles Peterson," told several people he was originally from Minnesota, was a ski and tennis instructor, and had come to Mexico for a new life after becoming estranged from his family. Chiapas, it seems, ended up being the perfect hiding spot for Addis and his new bride. Addis was able to immediately fit in under his new alias in a routine he'd repeated during the prior two decades, from California to Salt Lake City, Las Vegas to Florida and Guadalajara. He was accepted into Chiapas and Tuxtla Gutiérrez largely without question.

Addis, in fact, was so adept at adopting his new personality in Tuxtla Gutiérrez that he gained the confidence of a local police chief, who hired Addis to tutor his sons in English. Addis also picked up a job as a tennis instructor at the local Rustic Club—a posh, resort-type community featuring a golf course and numerous tennis courts.

He and Laura Liliana had two children. Their first, Etan

Peterson Padilla, was born shortly after they arrived in Chiapas. Their second, Itchel Peterson Padilla, was born three years later. The children were beautiful, sweet children, and local residents reported that Addis doted over them. He took them to the Rustic Club regularly to play tennis. However, all was not rosy in their family life, and some neighbors of the couple at their apartment complex also noticed Addis seemed to be very controlling of his wife.

On October 18, 2006, neighbors realized they hadn't heard or seen Addis, Laura Liliana, or their two children in several days. When they went to the apartment, they noticed a grotesque stench emanating from within. The apartment door was padlocked from the outside, and the windows were sealed.

The police were called and broke into the home, where they found a scene of absolute horror: Laura Liliana was dead on her bed. The children were both dead as well, their corpses found in their beds. Next to Laura Liliana's body, police recovered more than twenty syringes. Authorities believe Addis was injecting Laura Liliana with some type of drug, but it is not known which one. The Mexican State Agency of Investigation in Chiapas determined that the three victims died of "inhalation of carbon monoxide." It is not known to this day how Addis caused the apartment to be inundated with the odorless, colorless, lethal gas. Common sources of carbon monoxide fatalities in residences are usually attributed to faults or leaks in stoves, gas ranges, or heating systems.

The Mexican State Agency of Investigation conducted an intensive search for Addis in the area, but he was long gone. He'd vanished again. Their inability to find him,

the syringes next to Laura Liliana's body, and the method
of death led them to conclude all three victims had been
murdered. The local newspapers picked up the story and
summarized the horrifying crime scene for readers. The
Diario de Chiapas ran the next day's story under the head-
line, "The Whereabouts of the Father Are Not Known."

"Several lines of investigation are had; one indicates
a possible massive suicide," the paper reported in copy
translated by the author. "The rotting scent that emanated
[from] the house located in street twenty-one the North
West, in the colony the Paradise, of this capital . . . gave
warning to the authorities, that thus discovered the three
members of a family . . . dead. The [location of the] fourth
member of the family was not known. [He is] identified [as]
Charles Peterson, who . . . disappeared [on] Monday. The
hypotheses are several, one of them based on in question
possibility of a massive suicide, since to the interior of the
house were syringes."

A Mexican wire service agency reported across Chiapas that the "Elements of the State Agency of Investig-
ación is looking for the citizen of Canadian origin, Charley
Peterson, after the finding of corpses of his wife and her
two smaller children."

The Mexican State Agency of Investigation eventually
tracked down Laura Liliana's father, who was asked to
identify the body. He was apparently unaware he had two
grandchildren, who, like his daughter, had been murdered.
The agency, following in the footsteps of Las Vegas detective Larry Hanna, initiated a massive manhunt. Unlike in
Addis's prior cases, though, it wouldn't take long to find
him.

Weeks after the bodies of Laura Liliana and her children were found, a maid at a hotel room in Guatemala City received no answer to a knock on a door for a room she was responsible for cleaning. She knocked on the door again, got no answer, and entered to find a decomposed body in the bed of the room. Police were called and found multiple identifications in the room. One ID listed the man as John Charles Stone, age forty-six. A birth certificate for Stone also identified the man as having been born in Calumet, Michigan. All of the identifications were later determined to be fakes. The body was taken to a local coroner's office and an autopsy was performed. The cause of death for John Charles Stone was listed as heart attack, but it was unclear how long his deceased body had been in the hotel room before it was discovered or why it hadn't been discovered earlier.

The FBI also found in the man's possession "sports facility identification cards" and documents from the Mexican Social Security Institute that indicated he had a wife and two children in Chiapas. When the FBI investigated further, they learned the wife and two children had recently been found murdered in Tuxtla Gutiérrez.

The following is an FBI summary of the finding of the body and the investigation into the man's true identity:

John Patrick Addis, a fugitive who was wanted since 1995 for murder, kidnapping and other charges in the United States, was found dead in a hotel room in Guatemala City. The Guatemalan death certificate states he died of a heart attack and advanced putrification. Toxi-cology results are still pending. There were no reported signs of violence or forced entry into his hotel room.

Guatemalan authorities listed the name John Charles Stone, forty-six, on the death certificate, as they found several identification documents with this name and the corpse's picture in his hotel room, plus a purported Michi-gan birth certificate with a date of October 11, 1960. Authorities confirmed that the purported birth certificate and Social Security card in the name of John Charles Stone were fraudulent and that the Florida driver's license and Lee County voter's registration card in the name of J. Charles Peterson were also fraudulent.

After running LexisNexis index searches, [federal investigators] concluded that no such individual with that name and a similar age existed. As the individual also carried sports facility identification cards issued by the Mexican Social Security Institute for himself and an apparent Mexican wife and two children, which appeared genuine, [the FBI] asked Mexican Embassy colleagues for assistance in attempting to locate the wife in Chiapas. Mexican authorities quickly learned that all three family members had just been found dead in the house in Tuxtla Gutiérrez that they and Addis/ Stone shared, and he was the primary suspect in their murders.

We requested criminal records checks and learned through San Salvador that an individual wanted by police in Las Vegas, Nevada, had utilized the John

Stone alias, and had apparently fled to Mexico some ten years ago.

Las Vegas police detective Larry Hanna was quickly notified of the discovery, and his first reaction was to question whether it was really Addis. Could it be possible that he killed someone, placed the body in the hotel room, and then faked his death? It was possible, knowing Addis.

"He's that good at what he does," Hanna said.

But when fingerprints from Addis's stint as a state trooper were provided to authorities in Guatemala, the prints were a match.

"Las Vegas provided fingerprints and we were able to positively match them to prints taken from the body," the FBI wrote in police reports. "The FBI subsequently performed a formal match. The FBI's Las Vegas office provided contact information for one of Addis's sisters, permitting [federal investigators] to request necessary information for disposition of remains and preparation for the report of death. Post has requested an amended death certificate from Guatemalan authorities. Post assisted Mexican criminal investigators who needed to compare Mexican dental records with the body. In fact, as this is a high-interest case for them, they brought Addis's dentist with them from Tuxtla Gutiérrez and were able to definitively confirm that he was the same individual as their suspect in the Chiapas crime. Addis has been featured some six times on Fox's *America's Most Wanted* television program, so there was American media interest in the case."

John Patrick Addis was buried in Guatemala after the identification was officially confirmed.

24 ... CULT OF JOHN

Brent Turvey is one of the most respected criminal profilers in America. Turvey's a senior partner in Forensic Solutions LLC, and he's consulted with law enforcement and defense attorneys across America in some of the nation's most high-profile criminal cases. He offered many new and valuable insights on the evidence gathered against the so-called West Memphis Three case, which involved three teens convicted of brutally murdering three young children in West Memphis, Arkansas, in 1993. He's also done assessments of evidence in the JonBenet Ramsey and Laci Peterson murder cases, and Turvey is a nationally recognized figure on American television. He's an expert on multiple aspects of crime-scene investigation, including both physical and behavioral evidence relating to assault, fetish burglary, sexual assault, serial rape, domestic homicide, staged crime scenes, robbery and burglary, homicide, sexual homicide, and serial homicide. He agreed to provide

some basic thoughts on the fact pattern of the John Patrick
Addis case as presented to him.

Addis, he said, is not that unusual in being a cop who's
a domestic abuser.

"It is not unusual at all for law enforcement officers
to have multiple marriages, abuse their partners, and be
a gypsy with respect to their profession—moving around
a lot always [keeps them] one step ahead of being fired or
jailed," Turvey said.

The biggest thing about Addis that stands out for Turvey is the issue of control. Addis had to control everything
in his life out of a narcissistic desire to be worshipped by
those close to him.

"If . . . the fact pattern . . . is accurate, I am wondering
if there is substance abuse involved," Turvey said. "Essentially this is a guy with such low self-esteem that he needs
to control everything around him for fear of it leaving him.
And he's such a narcissist that he demands complete control,
attention, and compliance. [It's] like his family members
belong to a cult in which he is the head, and disobedience is
severely punished. Because he's a cop, he's trained to solve
problems by taking control or with violence."

Turvey compared the psychology of Addis to the mind-
set of leaders of apocalyptic cults.

Perhaps the most comparable is that of Marshall Apple-
white, who led forty members of the Heaven's Gate cult in
California to kill themselves in the belief that doing so would
get them on a spaceship to heaven. The members were all
found dead in a multimillion-dollar estate, wearing shrouds
with purple triangles on their chests. Observers said Apple-
white believed he and his followers were aliens on earth.

"I'm not sure the method of killing is unusual, especially

in the context of family killing, which is not unlike an apocalyptic cult in many instances," Turvey said.

"Maybe he was going to stage [the crime in Mexico] or something? Or this was his attempt at staging an accident?"

The questions remain for the families of the victims in Mexico and Las Vegas, and the unanswered questions are indicative of Addis's unique brand of criminality. He was a master at never being pinned down. He was an apparition of a man who wasn't who he seemed to be, and just when people started to figure out who he actually was, he evaporated and left and started over again to repeat his crimes elsewhere against good, unsuspecting people willing to trust and help a man who seemed to be completely normal. The ability of Addis to morph into a new person at each new stop in his life and to commit crimes without leaving behind evidence or explanations for his actions has left his victims' families with little relief from what Addis did. All have struggled immensely with the pain, suffering, and loss. Abbi Silver and Larry Hanna have talked to the family members in Las Vegas, and life will never be the same for them. Joann's daughters have been left forever without a mother, making Addis's crimes so hard to comprehend in their cruelty. Beyond that, Addis's decision to kill his own children in Mexico shows a commitment to controlling victims at all costs.

"I think he was a bad person to begin with," Silver said. "When you hear about how he treated his wife and four kids, he was a monster. He never changed. Just like you see with undercover detectives, they can lie really good. They can become another person. So you might meet a divorcée in [her] thirties, [she] may be a little lonely, so it's not that hard for John. He's an attractive guy. He knows how to play it.

"Evil and wicked: he just happened to be a state trooper," Silver said. "I'm not so sure that he didn't sit and think about Joann and plan it out. He was already so controlling, and there's a fine line between love and hate. Did he love her so much? Was this the one he couldn't have? The other women were mostly women who literally did whatever he said and eventually they left. Joann was a very strong woman who he could never control. That probably pissed him off: 'I'm pissed off because I can't control her,' and murder is the ultimate act of control," Silver said.

For Las Vegas police detective Larry Hanna, the Addis case is especially frustrating. He chased Addis for more than twelve years but never caught him. Addis was never brought to justice for four vicious murders. It was always John's way, and he controlled everything—not just women, but he was a rare criminal in that he was so intelligent that he was, in essence, able to control police investigations against him through his knowledge of crime scenes, evidence, and its destruction.

Hanna remains haunted by Addis's ability to avoid justice forever in this life, and the detective thinks about it often.

"It went on for years," Hanna said. "[From] 1995 to 2007, and on my desk I have these giant files of all these spottings across the country. John Addis is always there, and I ponder it a lot. I try to leave all this shit at work, but John was just one of those criminals who stuck with you. You'd see something on television or you'd hear something, and it would trigger the memory. Have I done everything I could? I knew that son of a bitch was south of the border . . . but we could never catch him.

"Anticlimactic is the only thing I can say," Hanna said.

"I worked this thing for twelve years; then, finally, they say he's dead. What else are you going to do? He's dead. It's the skills he'd developed as an officer and while living in Alaska and after that which protected him from justice. Lord knows where he's been and what he's done. A survivalist with urban skills. He can fit wherever he wants, and that makes for a very frustrating case."

ABOUT THE AUTHOR

Glenn Puit is an investigative journalist and policy specialist with the Michigan Land Use Institute in Traverse City, Michigan. He performs journalism that seeks to protect Michigan's natural environment. He also is responsible for communications and advocacy work on behalf of at-risk children in Michigan, and part of his journalism responsibilities include documenting rural poverty in the state. His work for the institute on energy and coal was recently submitted for consideration for a Pulitzer Prize in explanatory journalism.

Puit was born and raised in Lansing, in Upstate New York, and he graduated from Indiana State University with a bachelor's degree in journalism communications. Prior to joining the institute, he was a lead reporter for the *Las Vegas Review-Journal* for twelve years, where he covered violent crime and capital murder trials. While at the *Florence Morning News* newspaper in Florence, South

Carolina, Puit was the first reporter in the nation to identify John Doe #2 in the Oklahoma City bombing. The accomplishment was featured in *American Journalism Review*.

His first book, *Witch: The True Story of Las Vegas's Most Notorious Female Killer*, about the bizarre and gruesome case of matriarchal Vegas killer Brookey Lee West, was released by Berkley Books to national acclaim in 2005. The book was recently the subject of a cover feature story in the literary section of the *San Jose Mercury News*. His second book, *Fire in the Desert* (Stephens Press, 2007), is considered the evidentiary handbook for the Las Vegas homicide case of national bodybuilder Craig Titus and his fitness champion wife, Kelly Ryan. His third book, *Father of the Year* (Berkley, 2009), chronicles the case of Las Vegas double killer Bill Rundle, who was convicted of murdering his wife and mother. The book has been hailed as a true-crime masterpiece. His fourth book, *In Her Prime: The Murder of a Political Star*, is a moving and personal account of the poisoning murder of Nevada politician Kathy Augustine. His website is www.kingoftruecrime .com. He also communicates regularly with readers on Facebook and via his e-mail address, glenn@mlui.org.

Puit lives in Beulah, Michigan, and is the proud father of three children. In his spare time, he enjoys exploring the shorelines of Lake Huron, Lake Michigan, and his personal favorite, Lake Superior. He is also an avid fisherman who finds peace and tranquility fishing on Michigan's glorious rivers.

Penguin Group (USA) Online

What will you be reading tomorrow?

Patricia Cornwell, Nora Roberts, Catherine Coulter,
Ken Follett, John Sandford, Clive Cussler,
Tom Clancy, Laurell K. Hamilton, Charlaine Harris,
J. R. Ward, W.E.B. Griffin, William Gibson,
Robin Cook, Brian Jacques, Stephen King,
Dean Koontz, Eric Jerome Dickey, Terry McMillan,
Sue Monk Kidd, Amy Tan, Jayne Ann Krentz,
Daniel Silva, Kate Jacobs...

You'll find them all at
penguin.com

Read excerpts and newsletters,
find tour schedules and reading group guides,
and enter contests.

Subscribe to Penguin Group (USA) newsletters
and get an exclusive inside look
at exciting new titles and the authors you love
long before everyone else does.

PENGUIN GROUP (USA)
penguin.com

M224G0909